Textile Treasures
of the WI

Linda Connell

Anne Tranter

BRIGHTON 2008

'Textile Treasures of the WI'

First published in the United Kingdom in 2007 by
The National Needlework Archive
Boldre House, 5 Boldrewood Road
Southampton, Hampshire, SO16 7BW
www.nationalneedleworkarchive.org.uk
© The National Needlework Archive

Editor: Linda Connell

Photographs: Andy Brown, Romsey, Hampshire
Additional photographs under 'Photo Credits'
Printed by: Solent Design Studio Ltd
Claylands Road
Bishops Waltham
Hampshire. SO32 1BH

British Library Cataloguing in Publication Data
A catalogue for this book is available from the British Library

ISBN 978-0-9550790-1-6

The National Needlework Archive is an independent charity run by volunteers. Our aims are to document and preserve the textile heritage of Great Britain, to promote textile education, and to encourage contemporary work for public places. As well as the documentary archive, the NNA keeps a library of books, leaflets, patterns and magazines. Our Study Collection of textile artefacts includes teaching samples, worked textiles, sewing and knitting machines, laundry items, and a specific 'WI Collection' of banners, table covers and other related items. It is hoped that fewer artefacts are lost in the future with the provision of a collection dedicated to these community textiles. The NNA is financed entirely by donations and fund raising.

Foreword

It is an honour to be asked to write a foreword for this wonderful book and to acknowledge the tremendous work undertaken – on a voluntary basis – by all who have created the exhibition and publication. I speak on behalf of everyone who will see and read about these textiles when I say we are grateful to those who recognised the national importance of this Collection and who persevered in their work without financial support. They have shown us a glimpse of the needlework treasures held by the WI and by doing so have brought into sharp focus the need to preserve this invaluable national resource. This catalogue is a celebration of talent, a record of local and national history and an illustration of the development of textile design in the 20th century. It will inspire us to be creative and it will encourage us to take seriously our responsibility for the safety of these textiles. I emphasise their national importance and I say it is a shame that public funding was not available in the past to document and preserve them. I hope this may be remedied in the future. Please read the Conclusion carefully: we are all curators and these textiles are our nation's legacy to future generations.

Jennifer Wearden
Formerly Senior Curator [Textiles]
Victoria & Albert Museum

c.1920. Brasted WI. West Kent.
A year after their formation in 1919, the
members of Brasted WI decided to have a
banner. 'A lady in London' was employed to
design and make the banner at a cost of £10.
Appliqué in silk and cotton on linen.
Embroidered in cotton and wool threads

'Textile Treasures of the WI' Team

Linda Connell. Linda is the Director of The National Needlework Archive and wrote the text of the book with Anne Stamper. Linda organised the 'Textile Recording Project for the WI' through WIs and Federations nationally. She also researched and wrote the histories of the featured WI textiles and was Curator of the exhibition 'Textile Treasures of the WI'.

Pat Lumsdale. Pat is Head of the NFWI Unit at Denman College and Craft Adviser to the NFWI. Pat administered the NFWI part of the project and contributed to the 'fabric and technique' descriptions which follow the photo captions. Pat was responsible for the staging of the exhibition, with Sue Lewis, Suffolk East Federation.

Anne Stamper. Anne undertook the research into the historical aspects of the NFWI and wrote the text with Linda. Anne has been Honorary Archivist to the NFWI since 1999, and has written books and articles on aspects of NFWI history. A WI member since 1964, she has been a National Vice Chairman, and Education Adviser to Denman College.

Freida Stack. Freida was a volunteer with the NNA for the first three years of this project. She was responsible for the production of the initial version of the WI Textile Database. This involved reading through over 9000 documents and entering the relevant text details.

Acknowledgements

The project team would like to thank the following for their help and co-operation with this project:

The Boards of Trustees of the NNA and the NFWI.

The volunteer workers at the NNA who have worked on this project with dedication since its inception, and particularly to Con for his work and support.

The WI members and Federations who took the time and trouble to complete their recording forms.

The WIs and Federations who have been kind enough to loan their textiles for the exhibition.

Jennifer Wearden, the former Senior Curator (Textiles), Victoria and Albert Museum, for her encouragement and support of the project.

The members of Botley WI, Oxfordshire, for their help in assembling the recording packs, and Frank Stack for helping to unpack them on return.

Susan Winter, Joy Thomson and Con Connell for proof reading the text.

The WI members who have given their time to help with the staging and stewarding of the exhibition.

ICHF Ltd. for their generous sponsorship of the exhibition during its national tour.

Contents

Front Cover and Detail opposite:
Banner. The Needlewoman. 1924. Dormansland WI. Surrey

The Dormansland WI minutes for April 1924 state "Much interest was shown in the exhibition of the Institute's new banner which had been designed, worked and presented by Miss Chettle. It is a magnificent piece of needle and tapestry work which for originality of design and perfection of workmanship can be equalled in very few Institutes." Later that year the banner was exhibited at an NFWI exhibition at the Drapers' Hall, London. The woman depicts skills in handicraft and the cherries and blossom indicate the famous local fruit crop.

Silk embroidery on linen

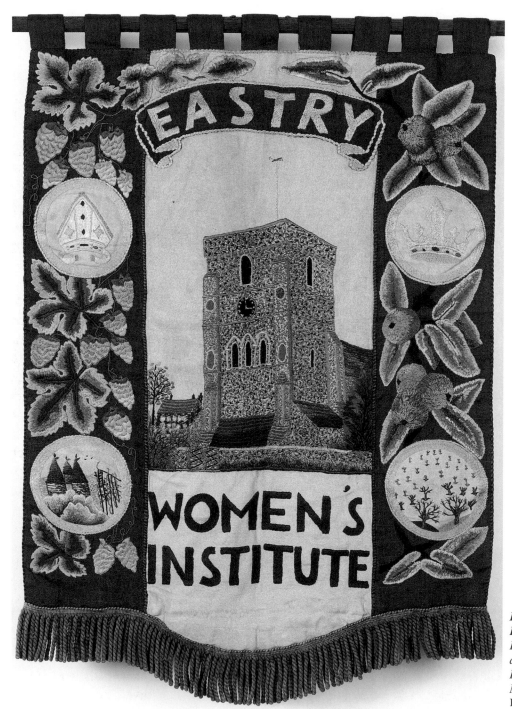

Banner. 1955, Eastry WI.
Kent East
Designed by Mrs Kate Brown and stitched by Mesdames Brown, Miller, Unwin, Clark, Marshall and Cork.
Embroidered in stranded cottons on linen fabric

Introduction

Textiles, in one way or another, have been at the heart of the WI movement from the beginning. Clothing, household linens and soft toys were at the forefront of WI activities and economic growth. Throughout more than 90 years of meetings, social gatherings, education, campaigns, and community involvement, textiles of some sort have been involved. Banners and table covers are immediately visible items which identify and unite WIs, but a wealth of other artefacts exist which harbour a national history, and which reveal the fascinating story of the WI. They also tell us about the WI's place in, and contribution to, Britain's culture from an exclusively female perspective. Textiles can be functional, or decorative, or both. Each of these aspects can make a different, but complementary, contribution to our heritage, and the range of items featured in this book are almost entirely women's work. This book's journey through the decades demonstrates not only the history of textiles within the WI but also reflects the changing emphases and styles within the wider community. This book accompanies a national exhibition which highlights the best, and the most representative, of this wide-ranging and fascinating textile collection.

The exhibition represents the end of the first stage in making a detailed, national survey of all the textile artefacts belonging to WIs in England and Wales, the Islands, the NFWI and Denman College. It is the result of a collaboration between the National Needlework Archive (NNA) and the National Federation of Women's Institutes (NFWI). One of the main aims of the NNA is to support and facilitate organisations such as WIs in monitoring and protecting their textile history and legacy, within the wider national context of ensuring the protection and preservation of the UK's diverse and invaluable needlework heritage. The NFWI were conscious that their own wonderful textile heritage, which had already suffered many losses, needed to be recorded and consolidated. The two organisations decided on a programme and the 'Textile Recording Project for the WI' began in 2004.

There are over 6800 WIs in the UK, grouped within 70 County Federations. Some Institutes are new, many go back for decades, but almost all have textiles which help to tell their story, of good times and bad, humorous and sad. To capture this wealth of local history required a massive effort. Each Institute was asked to complete a detailed recording form, describing all their textile artefacts and as much background information as was known about each. The items recorded had to belong to the WI, even if not made by members, and for the purposes of this particular project, it excluded items made by members which did not belong to the WI itself. To date almost two thirds of WIs have recorded their textiles with the NNA. Most were overwhelmingly supportive of this endeavour. Some WIs and Federations have not yet responded, and some WIs responded saying they had no textiles when we know from other sources that they do. Often this is a result of them thinking "we have nothing worth recording." However, from the point of view of a national survey, looking at trends as well as actualities, *everything* is important. Things often become interesting because of their collective, rather than their individual, presence. A single table cover may not, of itself, be remarkable; the fact that it is one of a hundred similar table covers might be. The project is on-going and the NNA will continue to collect this information until we reach our goal of 100% coverage.

Over 9000 forms have so far been returned. Each needed to be carefully registered and catalogued, and a picture of WI textiles across the country began to emerge. Perversely, the most immediate and obvious result is to see how much has been lost. Many items which we would expect to be there from written, photographic or oral evidence, have disappeared. From statistical trends we can tell that large numbers of banners alone, have been made, used, and vanished without trace. At the same time, it became clear that while some textiles are very well cared for, others are at substantial risk. Do things need to be valued before they become valuable? We often find it difficult to take seriously what is perceived as an 'everyday' item made by 'ordinary people'. Textiles are especially susceptible to this view but our generation is only the 'trustee for the time being' of these items and it is our responsibility to preserve them for the generations to come. Many of the textile pieces recorded are exquisite, in terms of workmanship, design, or because of the narrative they carry, but all are beautiful in terms of the women who made them and their legacy to us today.

It is always difficult to decide what to include in an exhibition. With many hundreds of lovely textiles to choose from, it inevitably meant that lots of wonderful items had to be excluded. The demands of a travelling exhibition such as the one envisaged for the 'Textile Treasures of the WI', using exhibits borrowed from WIs all over the country, made this task even more challenging. So the main criterion used was that each piece should help to tell the story of the WI through its textile heritage, which meant sometimes using the most revealing, rather than the most beautifully worked, pieces. Nevertheless, each piece is a 'treasure' because it takes an important place in the WI story. This criterion also meant that, in telling this story, some parts of the narrative would overlap, and some parts would be missing. The book and the exhibition have been structured in a way which maintains coherence in the overall picture, whilst at the same time highlighting aspects of particular interest or importance. The various sections in the following pages reflect these aspects – badges and banners, education and industry, home and country – in an attempt to show some of the ways in which textiles carry the histories of individuals and organisations over time.

This project would have been impossible without the help of the many Institute members who filled in the recording forms. Many saw this as (yet another!) chore, and this was reflected in their responses. But many seized the opportunity to celebrate and share what they knew, and what our request had prompted them to subsequently discover, about the textiles in their stewardship. Long telephone conversations with the NNA have since extended and clarified many of these records to give detailed and valuable resources for the future. Wherever possible, we have tried to validate the data the WIs have supplied, but inevitably we have relied heavily on their researches for many of the dates, photos and histories that have helped bring these textile treasures to light, and the stories about them to life. Where inaccuracies occur, it is to be hoped that these will be brought to the attention of the NNA so that our records can be amended.

WI Exhibitions

The exhibition, to which this book is a companion, is the most recent in a long line of craft celebrations by the WI. At local, Federation and National level, the exhibiting of work has been fundamental in demonstrating achievement, raising standards, and encouraging participation. The exhibitions have often been held in very prestigious places, and have frequently been visited by members of the Royal Family, giving the events a high profile and increasing popular interest. Textiles have always been a major feature in all WI craft exhibitions. As the exhibitions changed from being little more than large 'bazaars' to more ambitious displays, some even incorporated fully furnished rooms.

The range of goods on display at exhibitions has reflected the changing fashions and economic climate. In the 1920s and 1930s, when WI members lived in rural areas that were often still without electricity or piped water, many of the items were very practical: rugs, upholstery, spinning and weaving, and millinery. During the 1940s and 1950s, in times of war and post war austerity, again there were practical thrift items. Later, the items became more decorative, but toys, clothing, and household items have regularly been popular exhibition entries, and the fine quality of the workmanship has always been a feature of the judges' and visitors' responses. In more recent years the exhibitions have also been opportunities to display examples of what are now declining crafts, with an emphasis on passing on skills and expertise. The following pages highlight some of the notable exhibitions that have taken place over the decades.

Travelling Exhibition
Oxford 1923

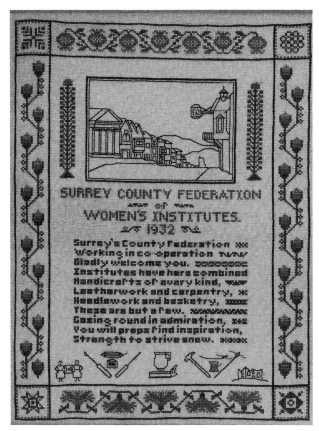

Sampler. 1932. Surrey FWI
This sampler has a rhyme about a WI handicraft exhibition and embroidered symbols of some of the crafts on show.
Cotton embroidery on linen fabric

National Exhibitions

1916. The first display of WI craft work was in June 1916. The Agricultural Organisation Society (AOS) took a stand at the National Welfare and Economy Exhibition in Hyde Park to publicise the work of the WIs. This was before the NFWI was formed and there were only a handful of WIs. Notable amongst the craft work were soft toys, especially a display of toy rabbits called 'Cuthbert' and these caught the attention of the press and the trade.

Cuthbert Rabbits

1918. Alice Williams, the NFWI Hon. Secretary, offered to organise an exhibition and sale to raise funds. The NFWI Exhibition and sale at Caxton Hall (which included garden produce and small livestock as well as crafts) made a profit of £330 for the central funds of NFWI. Banners were presented to the counties receiving the largest number of awards under selected classes. The very first edition of 'Home and Country' in March 1919 featured a photograph on the front cover showing Queen Mary and Princess Mary at the exhibition.

In the early days of Handicraft Exhibitions, banners were awarded as prizes for some of the classes. This banner was awarded to Sussex in 1918 for "best County Exhibit as a whole."

An Exhibition planned for 1919 had to be cancelled because of a rail strike – but there were many local exhibitions. A County Federation was formed as soon as sufficient WIs were opened in that county, and following the success of the 1918 National Exhibition, many Federations began to organise their own exhibitions and sales.

1918
Banner awarded to Sussex Federation

1920. In May 1920 The Second Annual Exhibition went ahead as planned, this time in the Royal Horticultural Halls, London. This exhibition was even more successful because there were now more WIs. Banners were again awarded to the highest scoring Institutes and the judges' standards were still very high. The judges' comments showed their objection to 'fancy work' reminiscent of bazaar items – which "does not do them credit as Institutes, and also is not saleable ...... mere fancy work, pen painting, crochet d'oyleys, and such like things being at a discount, and real industries being most admired and saleable."

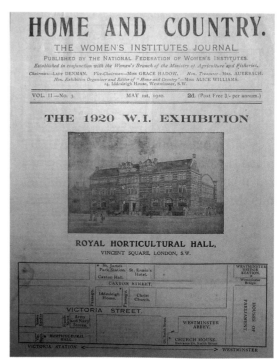

1920
Cover of 'Home and Country'

1921. A small display of craft work by the Guild of Learners at the Victoria and Albert Museum. Federations also put on their own exhibitions.

1922. The first National Handicraft Exhibition with only handicrafts, at the V&A. Space was limited and County Federations were asked to submit only 18 articles – only the finest specimens of work done by members – "the article must show as much craftsmanship as possible comparable with good taste". There were 652 exhibits from 49 counties and 281 exhibits from individual Guild of Learners members. The V&A only provided a small space and "If the space accorded us turned out to be too limited, this was partly caused by the crowd and crush of visitors which greatly exceeded all calculations".

Included in the exhibition were banners, pictures, smocks, plain needlework, gloves, and weaving. There were no sales, no competitions and no prizes; its sole purpose was to display the best handiwork the movement could produce.

1924. The Drapers' Hall. Members were reassured that "This is a large building and will hold many hundreds of people". The photograph of the main display area certainly shows plenty of space.

1927. Indian Pavilion of the Imperial Institute. This was the first year that gold stars were awarded, 54 in total. HRH Princess Mary made an official visit, and then unexpectedly the Queen came later in the afternoon, and was given "a little silk smock for Princess Elizabeth".

There was a comment in one of the reports that "many of the stars were awarded to work done in cottage homes".

1921
East Kent Touring Exhibition

1924 Exhibition
Bedroom display at The Drapers' Hall

1924
The Drapers' Hall

1929. This was the first exhibition to be staged in two venues, at The Imperial Institute South Kensington London, and then at the City Art Gallery in Leeds. There were 1,786 entries, 1,061 were displayed and 45 gold stars awarded. It was at this exhibition that a specially made Queen's Quilt was given to Queen Mary.

1932. The New Horticultural Halls, Westminster. This was the first exhibition where every County Federation submitted entries. Included were seven county co-operative rooms.

1935. The 8th Handicraft Exhibition organised by NFWI was held again at the New Horticultural Halls. 25,000 people visited in the week it was open. Exhibits were selected from entries from 57 County Federations. Mrs Heron-Maxwell, Chairman of the exhibition, wrote in the Foreword to the exhibition catalogue:

"….. The Exhibition shows more than 1,500 examples of work in 38 crafts, traditional, thrift, household and decorative, and the judges have given sympathetic consideration to the development of design on modern lines. Co-operative work is a feature of this exhibition; and the class for County Federation Loan Collections, intended to serve as models for beginners in the WIs, should be specially interesting to visitors.

The high standard of work shown in this Exhibition is largely due to the aims which, from the beginning, the NFWI has striven to uphold, namely, (i) to regain the practice of home handicrafts with a view to restoring the best traditions of English workmanship, (ii) to assist in bringing the best instruction in hand-crafts within the reach of the villages."

1938. New Horticultural Halls, Westminster (held just after the Munich crisis.) Over 40,000 people visited the exhibition, which was staged by Alice Armes, NFWI Handicraft Adviser.

Both HM the Queen and Queen Mary visited, and the Queen was given a work box for Princess Elizabeth made by Miss Averil Colby.

1932 Exhibition visited by Queen Mary
Mrs L.K. Huxley, Lady Denman, H.M. the Queen, the Countess of Listowel, Mrs Heron Maxwell, Miss Alice Armes

1938 Exhibition
Queen Elizabeth with Miss Somerville

1938
Averil Colby with the workbox she had made for Princess Elizabeth. Miss Colby is wearing a Guild of Learners' badge with ribbon

No exhibitions during Wartime

1946. Leamington Spa regional exhibition 'Craftswomen at Work'. It consisted of continuous practical craft demonstrations including spinning and weaving, gloving, toy making, patchwork, slipper making and three types of embroidery as well as plain sewing related to lingerie and upholstery work.

1952. Exhibition at the Victoria and Albert Museum with the theme 'Handicrafts in the Home'. The centre piece was the wall hanging 'Women's Work in Wartime', now at the Imperial War Museum.

NFWI decided to make this a smaller exhibition than the pre war ones and used area and county exhibitions to select the craft work to be displayed. Items were submitted for the county exhibitions according to the national schedule, those which received a minimum of 85% in the county judging were then sent to one of seven selection centres where the final choice was made for the exhibition. There were fewer restrictions than at times in the past; any material, any trimming, any method was allowed, but the standard of workmanship still had to be very high. About 700 articles were forwarded, out of which 500 were chosen for display.

1960. Exhibition at the Victoria and Albert Museum called 'The Country Year'. The Exhibition was professionally designed and staged and lasted for 20 days. The planning had started five years before when the Schedule was drawn up. It was circulated to counties in 1956 and they held their own exhibitions during 1958-9. At the county exhibitions 65,000 articles were shown of which 3,239 had marks of over 90% (or 95% for knitting). These items were forwarded to London for the selection centre committee to choose the 543 which would be exhibited. All selected were listed in the catalogue but not all were displayed.

1952
Making the 'Women's Work in Wartime' embroidery

Detail from the 'Women's Work in Wartime' embroidery

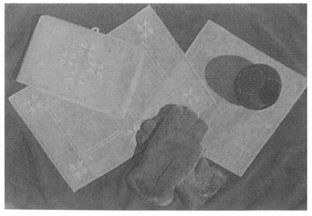

1960
Gifts for presentation to royal guests at 'The Country Year' exhibition

1965. To celebrate the NFWI Golden Jubilee, 'The Countrywoman Today' exhibition, which included handicraft items, was held at the Ceylon Tea Centre in May. During the week of the London AGM, seven windows at Harrods store had displays of WI craft work.

1975. 'Tomorrow's Heirlooms' was held at the Commonwealth Institute. Much of the craft work had a modern look and there were more decorative crafts as these were considered the sort of items which could be passed on as 'heirlooms'. There were bedcovers, christening robes, embroidery, gold work, pictures, and decorated boxes.

1984. Stands at the 'Life and Leisure Show' at Olympia. Craft work was for sale and on show, and a sale of the quilts from the 'Community Quilt' project took place.

2000. The National Craft exhibition in 2000 was not held in London but at Tatton Park in Cheshire and was called the 'Millennium Craft Spectacular'. As in previous years, selection of items to be included was through Federation events, each of which was visited by the team of National selectors. The selectors saw 12,000 pieces of members' mixed craft work at Federations, and 800 were exhibited at Tatton Park.

2007. 'The Textile Treasures of the WI'.
A touring exhibition with The National Needlework Archive. Exhibits were selected from nearly 9,000 textile items belonging to WIs which were recorded by the NNA during the first three years of the 'Textile Recording Project for the WI'.

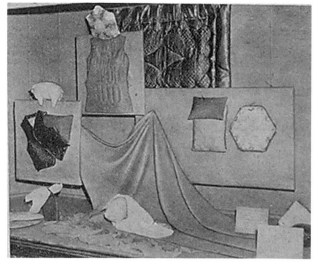

1965
NFWI Craft window display at Harrods

1984
The Queen at Olympia

2000
Selecting for Tatton Park

Textiles and the WI

The Women's Institute movement began in Canada with the first WI forming in Stoney Creek, Ontario in 1897. The first British WI opened in Llanfair PG on Anglesey, Wales, in September 1915. The women who joined this first WI, and the others that were soon to follow, were joining a radical new movement which would bring together all the women of rural areas in a way that had never happened before. The Llanfair PG WI was instigated by Madge Watt, working for the Agricultural Organisation Society (AOS). The AOS's primary aim at this time was to help to produce more food in war torn Britain, but they could see the value of the WIs, not only to individual women, who in the past had often lived very isolated lives, but also to the communities in which they lived. Textiles inevitably played an enormous part in the every day lives of these women. Clothing, household linens and furnishings were made, used, laundered and mended at home. Involvement with public organisations including the church, and now this new WI movement, also gave opportunities for women to use their design and needlecraft skills on more elaborate projects including table covers.

Buckinghamshire Federation County Rally late 1950s

Table Cover. c.1960. Kingston Magma WI. Dorset
Made by members of this Institute and used at monthly meetings.
Linen embroidered with stranded cottons

Badges and Crests

English Badge

Welsh Badge

1940s design

1950s design

As the movement became more established, WI members decided they needed a badge to give them a corporate image. They chose a badge based on that of the Canadian WIs with the same motto 'For Home and Country'. A rose was substituted for the left hand maple leaf to represent England, and the Welsh variant included a dragon. The design was quickly picked up for use on WI textiles and has been consistently used. It is still occurring on modern banners and table covers. The Llangyfelach banner features the 1916 badge but also has the updated 1930s logo underneath it with its simple, clear cut block design. This logo was soon softened however, with the 1940s and 50s versions. In 1953, Inez Jenkin's 'History of the Women's Institute Movement of England and Wales' was published, featuring a set of four woodcut designs by Reynolds Stone. One of these, with entwined roses, particularly caught the attention of WI needlewomen and has been a popular design ever since.

Table Cover. c.1953. Goostrey WI. Cheshire
This elaborately embroidered badge is taken from the 1916 design embellished with oak leaves, roses and ears of wheat.
Linen embroidered with silk threads and hand worked hem

Banner. c.1978. Llangyfelach WI. Glamorgan
*This banner shows the use of two badge designs.
The design surrounding the village picture is derived
from the earliest 1916 badge while the lower logo was
developed in the 1930s. The banner was designed by
Joyce Gambold and stitched by all members of the
Institute.*
Appliqué and hand embroidery

Banner. 1991. Hampshire FWI
*A modern banner, still displaying the very popular 1916
badge design, with Hampshire roses. It was made by
members of Hampshire Federation's Art and Craft sub
committee for a parade attended by Prince Philip.
Banner designed by Barbara Wells.*
Silk with hand applied satin, velvet and gold lamé motifs
edged in gold thread

Table Runner. 1954. Rowlands Castle WI. Hampshire
*This design, developed from the 1916 badge, shows the
rose for England and the maple leaf for Canada.*
Linen embroidered with stranded threads

Table Cover. Rauceby WI. Lincolnshire South
*Rauceby WI have a set of 14 of these cloths which were
purchased from Quarrington WI some years ago.
The rose pattern was one of the Reynolds Stone
woodcuts. The design is fairly common on WI textiles.*
Embroidered with stranded cottons on cotton fabric

In May 1955 the most successful design for WI textiles was launched in 'Home and Country' magazine, with the offer of a transfer in the style of a wreath made up of mixed tree leaves. The article was written by Constance Truscott "on behalf of the NFWI Handicraft Sub-Committee" but does not say who was responsible for the original design. The article recommended felt appliqué or white stitching on a plain background of navy, red, green or royal blue, and suggested that stitches could be taken from Mary Thomas's 'Dictionary of Embroidery Stitches' or 'Samplers and Stitches' by Mrs A.H. Christie. The transfer itself was available in two sizes and came with a sheet of three suggested working instructions. For the last fifty years this design has been consistently popular, appearing in all colours and styles. Hundreds of table covers, banners, book covers and other textiles have featured this design which still looks good today.

Banner. 1965. Whitstone WI. Cornwall
This banner was made by Mrs Meta Uglow for the Golden Jubilee rally in Cornwall in 1965.
Felt appliqué on cotton

Table Cover. Twyford & Ruscombe WI. Berkshire
This cloth was previously owned by Waltham St. Lawrence WI but no records survive as to its origins. The monochrome style was one recommended in the original working instructions with the wreath transfer.
Linen with cotton embroidery

Book Cover. 1965. Euxton WI. Lancashire
Made as part of the NFWI's Golden Jubilee Scrapbook Project by Elizabeth Balshaw.
Stranded embroidery cottons on linen

Table Cover. c.1960. Shrewton & District WI. Wiltshire
Mrs Betty Matthews embroidered this cloth, a little every day, while her husband did the washing up to enable her to have the time to complete it. Some years later, the cloth was damaged by mice at the village hall and some of the motif was destroyed. Mrs Matthews repaired the cloth, remaking both the fabric and the embroidery.
Linen with stranded cotton embroidery

Table Cover. 1972. Bardsey-cum-Rigton WI.
West Yorkshire
This cloth was embroidered by Sister Dorothy and Sister Helen Mary, both over eighty years old, of St. Hilda's Priory in Whitby. The linen was imported especially from Ireland and the project was made possible by a bequest from a Miss Pearson.
Linen embroidered with stranded cotton embroidery thread

Table Cover. 1954. Sambourne WI. Warwickshire
The 1955 wreath design is used in many different ways such as in this split pattern. The linen for this cloth was purchased by Kath Crump 50 years ago and she was still the WI treasurer in 2004! It has been in use at all WI monthly meetings since it was made by Miss Crump, Mrs Hadley, Mrs O'Shea and Mrs Hallam.
Linen with stranded cotton embroidery

Table Cover. 1965. Morton WI. West Yorkshire
Presenting the new cloth made by Mrs Marjorie Wilkinson (on the right) to the Institute in 1965.
Felt appliqué on green baize with couched cords to border

As Federations were formed, they too developed their own emblems, generally incorporating County or National symbols. Some examples include Welsh Federation badges which often have a dragon, Buckinghamshire's Swan, Kent's White Horse, Worcestershire's Worcester Black Pear, and the red roses of Lancashire and Hampshire. The Lincolnshire North Federation cloth incorporates ears of corn which lend themselves very nicely to gold embroidery. Individual WIs have also adopted County symbols for their textiles.

The WI tree logo was introduced in 1977 as a trademark for WI Books but was soon adopted as the NFWI badge. It has not been widely used on textiles, the older, more decorative designs still being more popular.

Table Cover. 1975.
Parkfield WI.
Isle of Man
Parkfield WI have had this cloth since soon after their formation in 1974. Made by members of the WI it shows the famous symbol of the Isle of Man.
Cotton embroidered with stranded cotton

Picture. 1990.
Lincolnshire North FWI
The picture features the modern tree logo of the NFWI. It was made for a competition in 'Home and Country' by Jane Blenkhorn.
Mixed applied fabrics with hand and machine stitching

Table Cover. 1991. Ceredigion FWI
Each of the six side panels on the cloth was embroidered by one of the six groups within the Federation. The centre panel is the Federation badge. The lettering shows Welsh at the top of the cloth with English along the bottom.
Embroidery on linen, appliquéd onto Welsh wool cloth

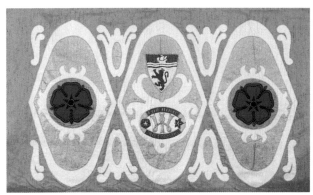

Table Frontal. 1970. Devon FWI
Federation table cover designed by Mr. James Paterson,
ARCA and made by Mrs Watkins, Mrs Levens and
Mrs Brasil.
Applied cotton and lamé fabrics on padded dupion

Table Cover. 1997. Lincolnshire North FWI
This Federation table cover was made by Helen Snee and
fellow WI members to celebrate 100 years of the WI and
20 years of Lincolnshire North Federation.
Heavy dupion embroidered with appliqué and goldwork

Table Frontal 2001. Gwent FWI
This Federation frontal features a ship called a Llandogo Trow.
Appliqué and Hand Embroidery on Velvet

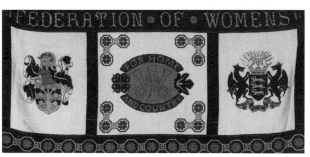

Table Cover. 1959. Cumbria Westmorland FWI
Federation cover designed by Mrs W. Wightman of
Crosscrake WI and worked by over 100 WI members.
Wool cross stitch on linen

In 1975 the National Federation was awarded a coat of arms to mark its Diamond Jubilee. It was designed by J.P. Brooke-Little, MVO, MA, FSA, Richmond Herald at Arms, and stitched by members of Kent West Federation.

Mr Brooke-Little described the coat of arms in the following way; "The Bar Dancetty and the Pallet are ancient heraldic charges which happily form the letters WI. The pierced suns are a pun on Lady Denman's maiden name of Pearson and are also symbols of education, energy and light. The lion in the crest is quartered in the Welsh colours and may be taken to represent England and Wales. It is hardly necessary to state why it holds a distaff. The heron supporters were thought to be elegant symbols of the countryside and are associated with all the elements as they fish in the water, nest on the land and fly in the air. To distinguish them from other herons, they stand among reeds."

A transfer for the coat of arms was offered in 'Home and Country' in 1978, since when it has appeared on many different WI's textiles – if the WI had an accomplished needlewoman prepared to undertake the task!

Book Cover. 1990.
Hutton WI. Essex
File cover for the President's file. Made by Mrs Eveline Hose and Mrs Joy Buckley for Hutton WI's 70th birthday.
Embroidered with stranded threads on linen

The development of the WI badges can be seen through their use on a variety of textiles. However, using badges to date WI textiles for which there are no written records can be problematic. As the old badges are still being worked on modern items, the item's date can only be said to be 'not before' certain designs were introduced. Table covers featuring the leaf wreath design, for instance, would not have been embroidered before 1955, but they may be much later.

However, the changing designs and styles of the badges and emblems through the years can be traced on these beautifully embroidered artefacts.

NFWI Coat of Arms Table Frontal
Used at the NFWI's AGM and other special occasions, the frontal was made by members of West Kent Federation.
Hand embroidery on linen

Banners

Banner Parade at the Buckinghamshire Federation County Rally at Hamden House. 1947

Banners were among the first institutional textiles made and used by WIs. Most organisations of the 19th century would have had banners to declare pride in their identity and to act as a beacon for organisational solidarity. Many of the WI leaders had been involved with the suffrage movement and were familiar with banners. Grace Hadow, the first vice chairman of NFWI, had been at Oxford in 1907 when the Women Students' Suffrage Society was founded and she had reportedly followed its magnificent banner in the great procession of 1908 to the Albert Hall.

It was a natural progression for the newly formed WIs to make themselves banners. In the 1918 NFWI Handicraft Exhibition at Caxton Hall there was a class for Design of Banners. This class was judged by Captain Kettlewell and he commented that generally the banner designs were not bold enough for "out of door pageant". In an article about banners for the March 1923

'Home and Country' he also stressed the need for a banner to be seen clearly enough to fulfil its purpose of identifying the group to which it belonged.

"...in designing a banner for a Women's Institute, the first consideration is a statement such as: "Neatey-cum-Handy Women's Institute", set out in clear, well spaced lettering being capable of being read at, say, twenty five yards. Letters about three inches high will be found appropriate."

He goes on to give advice on size and colour, "the size is fixed eventually by what can be carried conveniently by an average woman in a wind"- quite a different requirement to trade union banners which could be up to sixteen by twelve feet in size. He concludes "Let it be remembered the chief considerations in a banner are legibility, form, colour and material."

By this time it is clear that WIs and Federations were making banners which were used in processions. In 'Home and Country' November 1920 there is a description of a Craft Guild Procession:

"This procession was arranged jointly by the Learners' Guild of Home Crafts and the West Kent Federation of Womens' Institutes. Representatives from eighty Women's Institutes in West Kent marched in procession with music and flying banners, in order to testify their faith in home crafts as a means of self education and self expression, and in the home-maker as the real builder of a reconstructed empire."

Buckinghamshire Rally 1934

Reports in 'Home and Country' show that banners were widely presented as prizes in 1920. For example, in Staffordshire at their first County Federation Exhibition "Lichfield WI carried away the beautiful banner presented by our President Mrs Harrison OBE to be held for a year by the Institute gaining the greatest number of awards" and at the Shropshire Federation Exhibition held in Shrewsbury "..banners and certificates were presented."

Banners were also given for other fields of special endeavour. At the AGM in 1921, banners were presented to those who had raised the most money for the endowment fund in the previous year. This was money raised to help the NFWI become independent financially when the government grant was finally withdrawn. West Kent received the banner for the County Federation which had raised the most in 1920 (£405 15s 6d), and Cowley WI, Middlesex, raised the most, (£59 15s. 0d.), as an individual WI.

Banner. 1923.
Aston & District. WI.
Cheshire
Couched cords and braid with applied letters on linen

Banner. 1920. Cowley WI. Middlesex
One of Cowley WI's fund raising events was a fete where over £50 was raised and sent to the NFWI Endowment Fund.
Made by Toye & Co., London.
Two shades of gold silk embroidery on linen

To help increase subscription numbers, in 1922 banners were given to WIs where over 50% of their members took 'Home and Country'. In 1923 banners were awarded for 75% membership subscription. By 1924 banners were awarded for 100% subscription. These banners were made by members of the NFWI Handicraft committee and the design changed each year.

Banner 1924. Renhold WI. Bedfordshire
Thought to have been in its frame since 1924, the banner is now showing some sunlight damage.
Silk embroidery on linen

At the NFWI Handicraft Exhibition in 1924 at the Drapers' Hall there was again a class for banners but 'Home and Country' reported that while every Institute should have a banner, they should be "representative of some endeavour" and the ones on show did not meet with much favour from the judges: "The banners were the poorest of all the exhibits…. Carried at the head of a gathering representative of a particular institute, the banner should stand for the institute ideals which every member has at heart. A county Banner should signify the great united effort of the Federation"

However by the 1927 exhibition those banners on display "were praised as good examples."

Banners show individual designs to reflect the locality or folk lore and some even use significant material. One made in 1938 by

Crawley Hill WI, West Sussex, was made from a piece of blue and gold brocade that draped the royal box at the coronation of George VI in Westminster Abbey. Many different fabrics, styles and techniques have been employed to make the banners, and they reflect the expertise of the members at the time who were prepared to take on the job of making the Institute banner. Unlike many trade union banners which were commercially produced woven silk or painted banners, most early surviving and modern day WI banners are embroidered. Painted banners are unusual in the WI where needlecraft skills have always been highly valued. There have been painted banners, but the constant handling and rolling of banners for storage means that painted banners, which have a tendency to crack, have not survived as well as their stitched counterparts – especially early WI banners which may have been in regular use for up to 85 years.

Banner. 1954. Llangorse WI. Powys Brecknock
Designed by Mr. Norman Glover and made by
Mrs. Glover.
Painted design on coarse cotton

Canvas work banners have always been popular as they enabled a large number of members to contribute to the making by putting in a stitch, and they are very hardwearing. Guidelines have been given by the NFWI over the years on banner design and construction, and classes offered at Denman College.

Banner. 1957. Rayleigh WI. Essex
The members of Rayleigh were inspired to make a pictorial banner by the 'Women's Work in Wartime' embroidery. Designed by sisters Joy Cotton and Lorna Poole, it was stitched by them and 18 members of the Institute. The banner won a special award at the Essex Handicraft Exhibition in Chelmsford in 1957.
Wool canvas work

Church days and village fetes, giant picnics and similar community occasions would always see the local organisations parading and showing off their banners. Nowadays this is a much rarer sight and banners have ceased to be so visible. However, they are still produced and used for WI meetings and Federation functions.

WI banners have flourished and displays of massed banners are always very impressive.

1965 Federation Banners on show at the Albert Hall to celebrate the NFWI's Golden Jubilee

Banner. 1989. High Wycombe WI. Buckinghamshire
*Designed by John Gore and Mrs N.Simmons, the banner
was made by Mesdames Gore, Simmons, Long and
Wood. Princess Diana visited and was very interested in
the making of the banner.*
Appliqué and embroidery

Banner parade 1947 Buckinghamshire

Banner. 2000. Avon FWI
*This banner was made to celebrate the 25th anniversary
of Avon Federation. It was designed and made by ten
members of the Federation. The rays show the work of
the Federation sub committees – Organisation,
Environment and Public Affairs, Combined Arts, Home
Economics, Sport and Leisure, Education and Finance,
and Office.*
Embroidered appliqué on dupion fabric

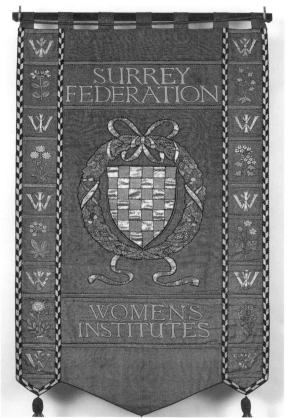

Banner. 1927. Surrey FWI
*Each of the Surrey WIs in existence at the time
contributed 1/2 d towards the cost of the banner which
was designed by Miss Joan Drew. It was made by
members of Blackheath, Chilworth and Shalford WIs,
and the materials cost £6 8s.0d. At some time the gold
thread work was renewed by Miss Catherine Bullock.*
Embroidered wreath with gold laid-work ribbon and shield.
Surrey wild flowers to side panels, black couched cord.
Lettering in gold cotton-a-broder on linen ground

Banner Parade

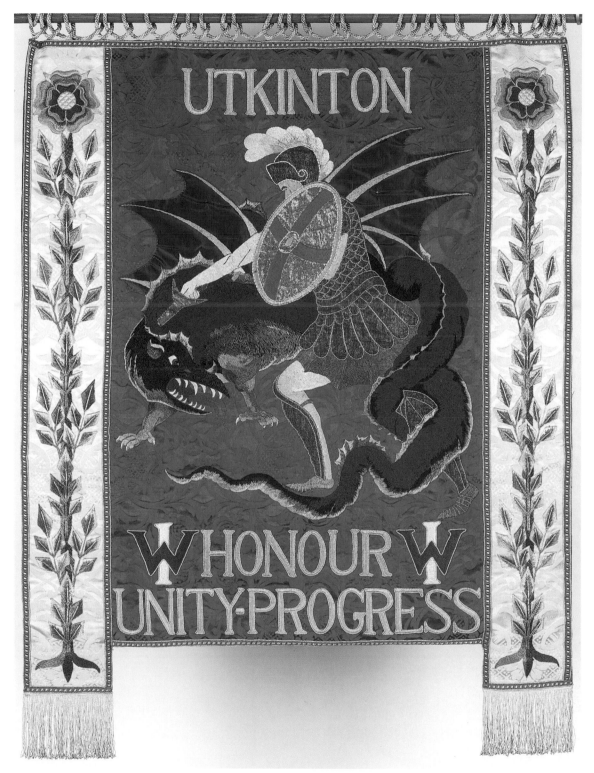

1937. Utkinton WI. Cheshire
George and the Dragon, made by WI member Miss Blair with the side panels designed by Miss Lois Prestwich.
The banner was presented by Mrs Rene Prestwich who was the oldest member at the time and who had, in 1923,
donated the hall for the WI to hold their meetings.
Embroidered in silk on brocade

Meanwood WI. West Yorkshire
Probably made shortly after the formation of this Institute in 1919. The owl represents Leeds, and prominent are the white roses of Yorkshire.
Cotton and silk appliqué on linen

Banner. 1929. Norfolk FWI
Norfolk Federation Banner, made by WI members from 21 Institutes. The banner appeared at the NFWI 1929 exhibition and a picture of it was featured in a 'Home and Country' report on the event.
Appliqué and embroidery on cotton fabric

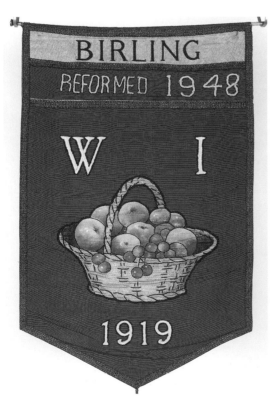

Birling WI. West Kent
Made by Miss Kiltke in the early days of Birling WI which closed and reformed in 1948 at which time the banner was altered.
Silk based banner with painted and applied images with hand worked tassels

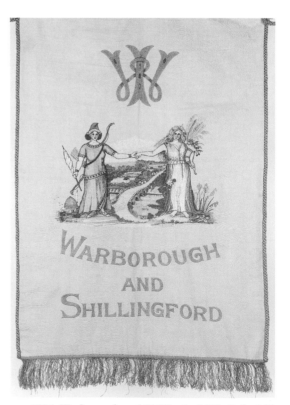

pre 1924. Warborough and Shillingford WI. Oxfordshire
Artemis and Demeter at Shillingford Bridge.
The banner may have been commissioned from a London firm by Mrs Greet. Having been stored in attics, cellars, garages and even been lost for a few years, the banner is in surprisingly good condition.
Linen embroidered with silk threads

1928. Cannington WI. Somerset
In 1926 a suggestion was put to Cannington WI that a new banner be made for an exhibition in Taunton. Members' designs were submitted and one was the outright winner. Members obtained the materials and stitched the banner, finishing in 1928 at a total cost of £5 11s 6d. In June 1930 the banner was sent to the exhibition in Taunton. Judge's note states – "An allegorical design is not suitable for a WI banner. Artificial silk unsuitable. Rejected." Fortunately, the members of Cannington WI held on to their banner.
Artificial silk appliqué with wool embroidery on linen base

1928. Huntingdon and Peterborough FWI
Commissioned by the Executive Committee of Huntingdon Federation, the banner cost £6 10s.0d. and was paid for by donations from WIs. It was designed by Mr. W. Whymper and made by Mrs Janet Garrod.
Canvas work in wool

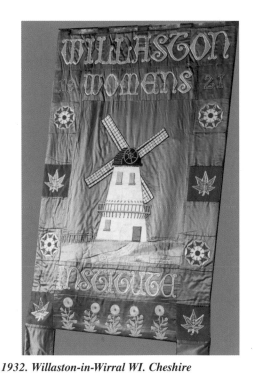

pre 1931. Marnhull WI. Dorset
Made by members of the WI Craft Group, the banner is first recorded at the back of a large group of people in a photograph dated 16th August 1930.
Linen appliqué outlined in stem stitch with black wool

1932. Willaston-in-Wirral WI. Cheshire
The banner was finished for a County exhibition at Chester Town Hall in October 1932 where it was awarded a 1st Class certificate. It was chosen to go on to the NFWI London exhibition held at the Royal Horticultural Hall in November 1934. Designed by Mrs Johnston, who ordered the specially dyed fabrics from Harrods, it was stitched by her and six other members of the WI.
Satin embroidered with silk floss. Maple leaves and roses worked on Glamis linen

1933. Eye WI. Huntingdon and Peterborough
Designed and made by Mrs Copeland, the banner records local landmarks of the day. The two windmills and the brickyard chimneys in the roundels have been demolished and the church now has a tower instead of a spire.
Cotton satin embroidered with silk threads

c.1935. Sutton Waldron & Iwerne Minster WI. Dorset
Although women of both villages belonged to the WI, the banner only shows the name of Sutton Waldron. This was because in the 1930s the Squire in Iwerne Minster did not approve the formation of a WI. The banner was probably made by the Misses Stephens.

1938. Radcliffe on Trent. Nottinghamshire
This banner was made by members of the Radcliffe on Trent WI Craft Guild for its first display at the County Craft Exhibition in September 1938. It gained 100 marks and went on to the NFWI National Exhibition, London in November of the same year.

1947. Cookham Afternoon WI. Berkshire
Made at the formation of the Institute in 1946.
Cotton appliqué

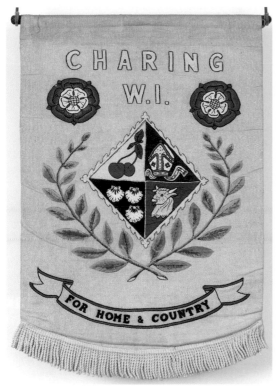

1953. Charing WI. East Kent
This banner was made to celebrate Coronation year and the design was chosen by competition within the WI. The winning design was by Mr and Mrs D.T. Bertram and it was made by 11 members of the WI.
Irish Linen with silk embroidery

c.1954. Llay WI. Clwyd Denbigh
This banner featured in 'Home and Country' magazine in the 1950s. Made by WI members, it was designed by Miss L. Evans and Mrs Helen Holmes.
Embroidery and appliqué on linen

1955. Thatcham WI. Berkshire
Thatcham is one of the claimants to being the oldest village in Britain. Designed by Mrs Fuller and stitched by WI members.
Cotton appliqué

c.1955. Glaisdale and Lealholm WI. North Yorkshire East
Miss H.M. Smith won an Institute competition with her banner design, which was then stitched by the members. The banner depicts a local legend about how the Beggar's Bridge came to be built and features the words of Lealholm poet Castillo who helped to build the Cam Bridge in Glaisdale.
Cross stitch on canvas with tent stitch edging

1965. Bledlow WI. Buckinghamshire
Made to replace an earlier, rather worn, banner. It was designed by Miss P. Whatmore and made up by her mother, who worked late into the night to get it finished for the Spring group meeting the following day. Several members helped with the stitching.
Appliqué and embroidery on cotton

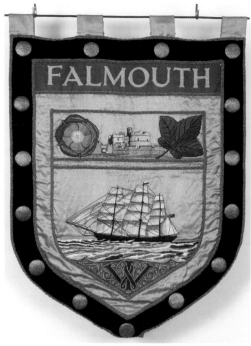

1965. Falmouth WI. Cornwall
This banner was made to mark the Golden Jubilee of the NFWI. In green and red with a black velvet border, it has the 15 gold bezants of the County of Cornwall around the edge. It features a Falmouth packet ship. Designed by Mr. R.E. West, it was made up by Mrs West with other members stitching the motifs.
Embroidered appliqué with couched braids on satin with a velvet border

1970. Thornton WI. Pembrokeshire
The design for this banner was the winner in an Institute competition. Designed and made by Evelyn Laugharne for a Pembrokeshire initiative for WIs to make banners. Of the 58 WIs in Pembrokeshire, 31 recorded having a banner but only 8 recorded having banners made in the 1970s.
Appliqué and embroidery on cotton fabric

1971. Oxwich & Penrice WI. Glamorgan
This banner is a copy of a stained glass window in St. Illtyd's Church, originally designed by F.W. Cole at the Swansea School of Art. It depicts St. Francis of Assisi. The banner was stitched by June Callaghan with other members of the Institute, and cost £16.90.
Felt appliqué with embroidery, couched black braid for leading

The Lee WI. First banner c.1924

1983. The Lee WI. Buckinghamshire
The Lee banner is a canvas work copy of the WI's original banner which was made in the 1920s. Straw plaiting was a local village industry. The original bonnet was silk with real straw plaiting but it was decided that the new banner would be easier for a large group to stitch if done in canvas work. Drawn out by Mrs Felicity Hilder with the stitches worked out by Mrs Betty Whitehead, several other members helped with the stitching.

1987. Chipstead WI. West Kent
Featuring local scenes and WI activities, this banner was designed by Anne Smith and worked by several members of the Institute.
Appliqué and embroidery on linen

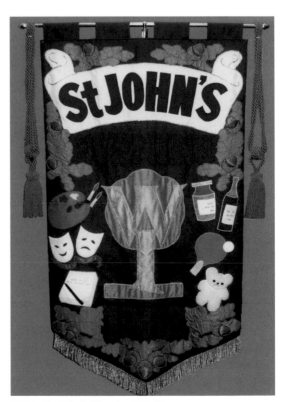

1993. St. John's Evening WI. Surrey
Made for the 30th anniversary of this WI and displayed, with many other Surrey banners, at the 75th anniversary service for Surrey Federation at Guildford Cathedral in 1993.
Machine appliqué. Mixed fabrics on a woollen background fabric

1994. Oxshott WI. Surrey
This is an accurate copy of an old banner which has now disappeared. The painted central panel depicts local landmarks and WI activities.
Painting, hand embroidery and couched braids on dupion fabric

2000. Alton WI. Staffordshire
Made by Mrs S. Delaney and Mrs S. Easter, the banner was made to celebrate both the Millennium and the 80th anniversary of Alton WI. Each member paid £1 to finance the purchase of materials and each member's signature appears on the front of the banner.
Appliquéd and quilted cotton

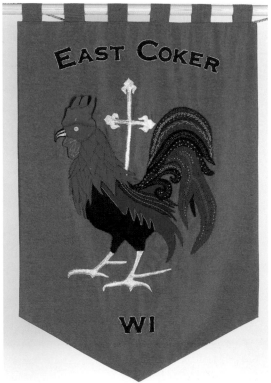

2003. East Coker WI. Somerset
The cockerel is the village crest of East Coker. The banner was made by several members of the Institute and designed by a 'WI husband'.
Felt and gold kid on dupion fabric

Uniform and the WI

From 1917 to 1919, the WI was under the direction of the Board of Agriculture and all its officials were entitled to wear the Land Army uniform.

In 1919, after the end of the war, it was agreed that "A uniform may be worn by regular and Voluntary County Organisers (VCOs), headquarters officials and officers of the County Federations." The uniform consisted of a brown corduroy coat and skirt with a white or brown silk shirt, a plain brown hat and a brown tie. It was supplied by Harrods for £3 8s. 0d. There was also a loose belted corduroy overcoat and a brown straw hat.

The story is told of one energetic WI Voluntary County Organiser, who had also been in the Land Army, who tried to get a WI formed in a village and to her surprise totally failed. It turned out that because the woman was wearing breeches that had not been seen much in those parts, the village women had thought that they would all have to wear them too!

The idea of a uniform did not last for very long. A member of the NFWI executive committee of the time explained that "'with the passing away of the war fever, the desire to wear uniform at any price has given way to the desire to look as nice as possible. Uniforms were greatly resented in my part of the world. Officialdom, especially if it happened to come from that south country place, London, was never popular and a uniform suggested officialdom."

1920
Lady Denman, the National Chairman, wearing the Land Army uniform as she returns from Buckingham Palace having received the CBE.

Uniform of a Voluntary County Organiser (VCO). Norfolk FWI
A modern reproduction in green corduroy. VCOs were renamed 'WI Advisers' in 2000.

First VCOs in uniform

However, it was felt necessary to be able to differentiate between representatives of individual WIs at Federation gatherings, and as a result WI name sashes came into use very early on.

Sashes are still used at Federation Council meetings and at the NFWI AGM. Some of the sashes are beautifully decorated and embroidered but few were recorded by WIs in the textile recording project.

Within WIs, badges of office are common, denoting President, Secretary etc. Sometimes these badges are more elaborate than a printed or enamelled badge.

Even though modern day WI members do not have uniforms, WI doll mascots are definitely dressed for the part. Many years ago a member of Frome WI made a doll from a wooden spoon for a local competition. The doll quickly became a popular mascot but eventually it wore out so it was decided to make a new one. 'Wilma' has been an interested and regular member of Frome WI since 2003.

Sashes. 2004
Members of Staffordshire Federation wearing their WI sashes at a Choral Evensong in Lichfield Cathedral to celebrate Staffordshire Federation's 85th Anniversary.

President's Brooch. 1994. Kendricks Cross WI. Lancashire
Cross stitch on Aida

'Wilma'.
Mascot Doll 2003.
Frome WI. Somerset
'Wilma' was made by Janet Blair.
Cloth doll, needle-cord suit and cotton blouse

Sashes from Gwent Federation
Marshfield WI. c.1970. Made by A. Medcalf, M. Wood and E. Osman.
Goytre WI. c.1990. Made by Mrs P. Roden
Caerleon WI. c.1996. Made by Mrs E.M. Bevan
Linen, cotton and silk with hand stitched motifs and embroidery in cotton threads

Topsy-Turvy Doll.
1993. Braughing WI.
Hertfordshire
Made by Rita Aitken.
The apron shows the 1897 date of the formation of the first WI in Stoney Creek, Ontario, Canada.
Jersey body, cotton clothes, hand and machine stitching

Table Cover. 1964. Meopham Nurstead WI. West Kent
Designed and made by WI members, the cloth depicts WI activities.
Linen with white embroidery in a variety of cotton threads with feather stitch motifs

Leisure Time

The monthly meetings of the WI are a focal point for members' practical and leisure activities.

The monthly meetings were designed to provide a vehicle for the improvement of rural women's lives. This improvement embraced the idea of making the most of leisure time, a concept alien to most hard working countrywomen. By focusing instruction, communal enterprise and social interaction on a regular group meeting, it was possible to provide a wide range of written materials, back up support, and trained tutors for both working and pleasure activities. The invited speakers would cover all areas of interest and give demonstrations, and the subsequent Institute classes and competitions encouraged hobbies as well as household skills. Institute textiles record these interests and show the type of activities that have taken place at WI meetings and events. The Albury WI banner, for example, demonstrates the equal importance given to singing, dancing and drama, as given to cleaning, baking and hen keeping!

Book Cover. 1995. Llandysul. Sir Gar Carmarthenshire
Designed by Mary Thomas and embroidered by Judith Roberts for a Carmarthenshire County scrapbook competition. The cover depicts the monthly WI meeting.
Hessian with applied cotton panel framed in felt and stitched in cotton threads

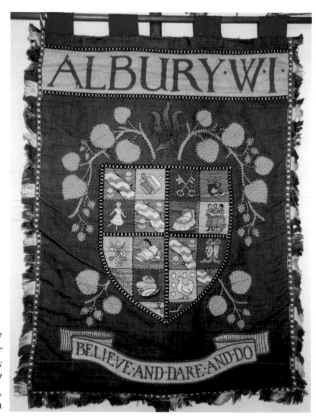

Banner. Albury Evening WI. Surrey
Previously belonging to Albury Afternoon WI, the banner depicts the local river and a range of members' activities including singing, dancing, hen-keeping, cleaning and washing!
Linen fabric with appliqué and couched details. Shield, satin stitch, long and short stitch

Communal social activities have also been addressed at the local Institute. As well as cultural pursuits, giant picnics were popular where whole families would be involved, as well as WI members-only days out where a few quiet moments could be caught to read or talk.

Wall Plaques. 1984. Gwynedd Caernarfon FWI
Part of the 'Women in the Community' set of wall plaques made for the Royal Welsh Agricultural Show, showing aspects of Health, Education and Community.
Canvas work using a variety of stitches and techniques in wool

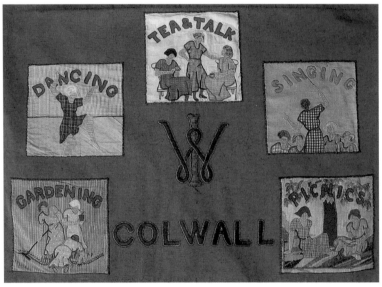

Table Cover. 1937. Colwall WI. Herefordshire
Five different activities are shown on this tablecover: Tea and Talk – an important part of WI life, – good speakers and companionship. Colwall WI archives state these occasions helped the women get through the difficult times of the war. Dancing – Colwall held regular dances in the 1930s. Singing – The choir was formed in 1937 and is still in existence. Gardening – In 1937 the WI took over the care of the War Memorial and they now maintain the gardens at the local railway station and have received a number of awards. Picnics – Giant County picnics for the WI took place in the 1930s and 1940s and it was for one of these that Colwall banner was used to head Colwall's part in the procession.
Cotton rep fabric with appliqué figures edged in buttonhole stitch

Table Cover. 1969. Smarden WI. East Kent
The cloth has 20 appliquéd panels, 12 depicting activities of the WI. Designed and made by 9 members of the WI for the 50th anniversary of the Institute.
Cotton with applied linen panels

Music and singing have played an important part in the year of most WIs, and members have used their needlecraft skills to work commemorative and celebratory textile items.

Banners, particularly, were used as prizes in music and singing competitions, and the Mickleover WI banner was won at Becket Street, Derby in 1923 for singing 'Dashing Away with the Smoothing Iron'. The Finsborough WI choral class, East Suffolk, the winning choir at the 1927 Singing Competition in Ipswich, were proud to posc with the banner they had won.

The Cumbria Westmorland Golden Jubilee Trophy for Craft demonstrates an unusual use of an embroidered item as a prize.

While music and other activities are regularly recorded on textiles it is heartening to know that fruit picking and jam making, often very enjoyable communal activities, are not forgotten!

Banner. c.1918. Mickleover WI. Derbyshire
Linen with Embroidery stitches over appliqué

1927. The Finsborough WI Choir. East Suffolk

Book Cover. 2000. Llanbister WI. Powys Radnor
This scrapbook was designed and made by Olwen Wilson for 'A Moment in Time'. Displayed at the County 'Pathway to the 21st Century' in September 2001, it gained 1st place in the category of Institutes having less than 30 members.
Needlepoint in wool on a felt background

Trophy. 1968. Cumbria Westmorland FWI
Presented every year after the County Show to the WI gaining the most points overall for Craft. Designed and made by Mrs W.M. Wightman.
Goldwork on silk

Hospitality

Welcoming guests, making them feel at home, and reaching out into the community are core objectives of the WI. Mottoes and homely phrases appear on samplers, wall hangings and table covers and remind members of the importance of working together for the common good.

Catering at the WI involves the niceties of life; well dressed tables, clean aprons, neat traycloths and embroidered cakebands. All are calculated to make day to day living special, and special occasions memorable.

Traycloth. 1981. Sanderstead WI. Surrey
In 1980 a £10 prize was offered for a President's traycloth with a Jubilee theme. The judging took place at the Sanderstead WI Jubilee luncheon in June 1981 and this cloth, made by Mrs Peggy Cole, was the winner.
Crochet in cotton

Tray. 2002. Penn & Tylers Green Evening WI. Buckinghamshire
Designed to commemorate the Queen's Golden Jubilee, the tray features designs from medieval tiles made in the village. Used as the Speaker's refreshment tray at meetings.
Cross stitch embroidery covered in glass

Ribbon Cake. 1999. Capel St Mary WI. Suffolk East
This cake was made by Mrs J. Simms and Mrs L. Bloomfield as a competition entry to the Suffolk Show, celebrating the 80th Anniversary of the Federation.
Woven Satin and grosgrain ribbons

Cake Band. 1998. Almondsbury WI. Avon
Mrs Sue Harris made the cake band for the 80th birthday celebration cake. Subsequently updated for the 85th birthday.
Cotton cross stitch on Aida

Apron. Scole WI. Norfolk
A set of 10 aprons used at WI catered events. Made by various members of the Institute, the embroidered patterns are different on each apron.
Cotton gingham with cotton perle embroidery

Book Cover. 1997. Thringstone WI. Leicestershire and Rutland
Photograph album for Institute events.
Painted WI logo on padded cotton with broderie anglais trim

Cushion. 1938. Sanderstead WI. Surrey
*'For Bone and Comfy'. The cushion was made
by C. Leech. It has a verse and musical notes
on the front and members names on the reverse.*
Hand embroidered on cotton fabric

Cushion. 1993. Northamptonshire FWI
*Made by Mrs Hazel Parsons of Barby WI as an
entry for the 75th Anniversary Craft Exhibition.*
Bonded cotton appliqué with couched cotton edgings

Embroidered Motto. c.1935. Hodnet WI. Shropshire
This motto was first displayed at the 21st birthday celebration of Hodnet WI in 1940. It was embroidered by Miss Manning.
Cross stitch on linen

Wall Hanging. 1998. Worcestershire FWI
*Designed and made by Di Chester of Whittington WI
for the Worcestershire Room at Denman College.
The panel features black pears which are the emblem
of Worcester and the Worcestershire Federation.*
Silk embroidery and painting on cotton fabric

Wall Hanging (detail). 2002. East Yorkshire FWI
*Made to commemorate the completion of the EYFWI
Millennium Orchard, the hanging shows 25 different varieties
of apple. 17 WIs in the Federation embroidered the apples and
the hanging was organised and made up by Mrs Lynne Taylor.
Presented to the Yorkshire Room at Denman College in 2003.*
Quilted cotton with fabric painting

When Denman College opened in 1948 there was still rationing and coupons were required for household textiles. Federations offered to help the College by furnishing bedrooms, and that tradition still continues. Of particular note are the quilts made for many of the bedrooms and these make the college rooms very special. The picture shows quilts being displayed on the Denman staircase in the 1950s.

Federation members also make wall hangings, cushions and workboxes for all the rooms at Denman to enhance the rooms and make a delegate's stay as pleasant as possible.

Cushion. 1999. Surrey FWI
Designed and made by Sally Dampney especially for the
Surrey Room at Denman College.
Moire fabric with embroidered motif on even weave linen

Patchwork Bedspread (detail). 1984. Suffolk West FWI
Made for the Federation room at Denman College by
WI members.
Hand stitched diamond patchwork applied to cotton base

1950s Quilts on Denman staircase

1950. A room at Denman College

2007. Room at Denman College

Table Covers

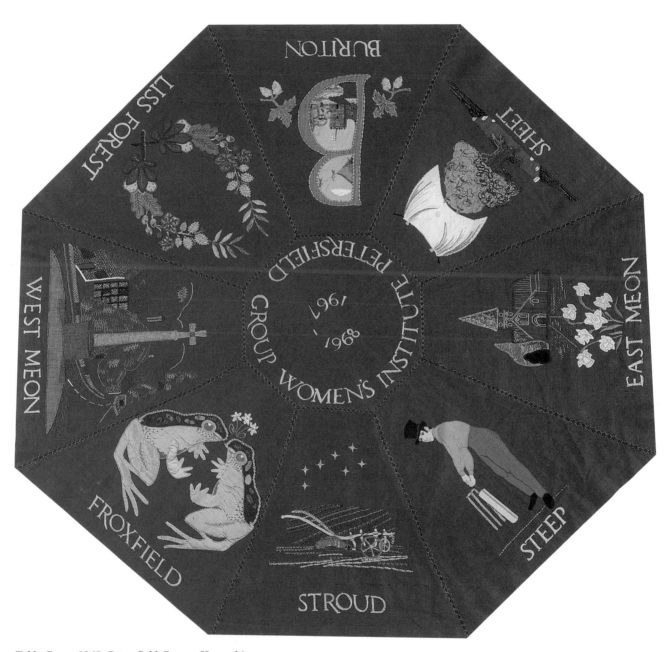

Table Cover. 1968. Petersfield Group. Hampshire
The idea for this cloth came from Mrs Doris Wright who was President of the Petersfield Group from 1967-68. Each of the 8 WIs embroidered their own panel. The cloth is now used by Petersfield Villages Group which includes Sheet and Stroud (now known as Stroud Afternoon), Stroud Evening (which meets in Steep) and West Meon. The symbols for each WI are: Sheet – Chestnut tree in centre of village, Stroud – farming with a pub called the Seven Stars, West Meon – stone cross, East Meon – local church, Froxfield – Natterjack toads local to the area, Liss Forest –WI leaf wreath, Steep – pub called The Cricketers, Buriton – church and Butser Hill.
Appliqué and embroidery on linen fabric

1954. Brailes WI. Warwickshire
The proud stitchers of Brailes sit with their new cloth. The cloth was designed by Miss Bramwell and stitched by all the members of the Institute. The circular pattern is 'The Warwickshire Shepherd' pattern.
Linen with cotton embroidery in white and two shades of red

c.1920. (detail) Brockham Evening WI. Surrey
Designed by B. Grace featuring birds and flowers.
Hand embroidery with cotton threads on linen

1985. North Curry WI. Somerset
The cloth features a Somerset Wyvern and was designed by Jane Urwich and members of the Institute. It has village scenes on the end panels.
Linen cloth hand stitched in perle thread with appliqué inserts and cross stitch lettering

Table Covers

Of over 9000 items initially recorded by the NNA in the Textile Recording Project for the WI, 5178 were table covers. Table covers are, therefore, the overwhelmingly most common type of textile held by WIs. Almost every WI has one. Even WIs who first responded that they had no textiles to record at all, almost always said "Oh yes, we have one of those" when subsequently asked specifically if they had a tablecloth for use at their monthly meetings. What is clear is that, although some are certainly cherished, very often these cloths are not regarded as being of any great value, either in financial terms or intrinsically. It is to be hoped that one result of the recording project, and its highlighting of the interest value of these items, will be to raise the appreciation of these under-rated, and often very poorly treated, heirlooms.

Heirlooms do not need to have a monetary value. They have a far higher status being carriers of memories from one generation to another. These are memories of events, people, cultural mores, and traditional skills. Where banners have served as identifiers and rallying points away from the meetings, table covers have come to fulfil the same purpose in the meeting hall. As the numbers of banners have declined with the decrease in outdoor events, the number of table covers has increased enormously. These cloths give a bright and colourful focal point, and often proclaim the WI name. This gives a sense of unity for members and shows their pride of place to visitors.

The following pages feature a selection from the table covers recorded. They are set out to demonstrate the changing design styles and techniques over the decades. Table cover designs have always been a lot more conservative than their banner counterparts. While design requirements, such as being able to distinguish it from a distance, and needing good use of colour, are the same for table covers and banners, table cover designs have tended to be more restrained.

The requirement to have something pleasant for members to stare at for two hours every month has perhaps constrained more outrageous designs. The following selection encompasses nearly 90 years, and it is interesting to see how some things have changed dramatically, and some things haven't changed at all.

The use of a table cover for improving the appearance of a plain table for dining was a well established practice when WIs started and this naturally spilled over into using a cloth for the President's table at WI meetings. Early WI cloths were good cloths brought from home, and were usually decorated with embroidery. Few WI cloths from this period survive today as they were generally thrown away or recycled when they wore out in the same way as other household linens. Once cloths started to be made especially for the purpose, they were often communal efforts and were shown off with pride both at home and at exhibitions.

The cloths made during the 1930s and 1940s show a move away from more traditional designs, and the introduction of simpler, bolder motifs and more colour. In the 1930s, designers such as Rebecca Crompton were starting to bring out the more modern, abstract designs that would be popular until the 1950s. Fruit motifs were common at this time, with the pomegranate as seen on Bearley WI's cloth being a consistently popular design motif, symbolising immortality and plenty. Medieval, sixteenth century and Arts and Crafts movement textiles have been high spots in the use of this pattern.

The use of felt was very common in the 1940s and 1950s. It is easy to handle and the lack of fraying meant a good-looking result for both the beginner and the more experienced stitcher. With more women having to decorate their own clothes and linens, felt was a popular choice of fabric. It was very suitable for appliqué on sturdy table covers as long as they didn't need washing, since often the wool would distort and the colours run. Design in table covers still saw the traditional in use alongside the more stylised patterns such as that on the Hurstpierpoint cloth. The more familiar 1950s design styles such as that seen on the Warwickshire sample book cover were apparently not popular for WI table covers.

Sample Book. 1950s. Warwickshire FWI
An embroidery teaching aid, the book forms part of a craft loan collection.
Cotton fabrics with hand and machine embroidery on card mounts

The 1960s and 1970s saw the use of plain colours and very one dimensional, bold designs. Flower patterns were simple, and gold kid was very popular.

By the 1990s, the album type, segmented design, had become widespread. This style of construction lends itself well to communal participation, but often the overall designs of the cloths lack focus and coherence. The Lockswood WI and Neatishead WI table covers demonstrate two methods of successfully unifying a segmented design.

All of the table covers in this chapter show the variety of fabrics and techniques employed to ensure that the top table at WI meetings looks pleasant and welcoming. The styles and colours are diverse, making each cloth individual and interesting.

1928. (detail) Grayshott WI. Surrey
This cloth was designed by Mrs Trollope who obtained the transfers. The individual panels were made by many WI members. Each panel is hemmed and they were then joined together.
Linen worked with cross stitch panels in blue stranded cotton joined with faggoted seams

1929. (detail) Portinscale WI. Cumbria Cumberland
This cloth was made by 8 WI members for the NFWI Handicrafts exhibition in 1929. It has been in regular use, with frequent laundering ever since.
Linen squares embroidered with silks, joined together with crochet

1929. (detail) Backwell WI. Avon
Made by members of Backwell WI to celebrate the opening of their WI hall, the cloth was exhibited at the NFWI Handicrafts exhibition in 1929.
Heavy cotton twill fabric with wool work embroidery

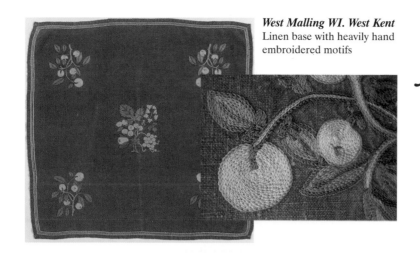

West Malling WI. West Kent
Linen base with heavily hand
embroidered motifs

A Celebration
of
Table Covers

Hurstpierpoint WI. West Sussex
No records exist about this lovely cloth.
Natural linen with hand embroidery in a variety of stitches

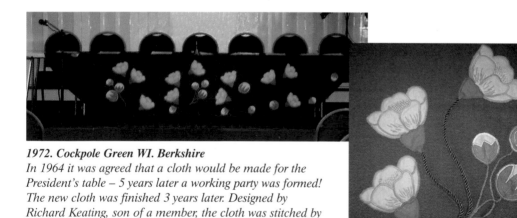

1972. Cockpole Green WI. Berkshire
*In 1964 it was agreed that a cloth would be made for the
President's table – 5 years later a working party was formed!
The new cloth was finished 3 years later. Designed by
Richard Keating, son of a member, the cloth was stitched by
Miss MacDonell with Mesdames Bendell, Wilkinson,
Romaines, Windle and Watson.*
Linen flowers appliquéd onto hopsack with couched cords for stems

2004. Bengeo WI. Hertfordshire
*Depicts local church and
flowers. Designed by Enid
Grattan- Guiness and made by
her and Julie Walsby with
Barbara Payne.*
Appliqué letters with hand and
machine embroidery

c.1935. Lydbrook WI. Gloucestershire
This cloth was made by Miss Muriel Smith who was President of Lydbrook WI before, during, and after the Second World War. Miss Smith gave the cloth to the WI when she left the village. It has been in regular use ever since.
Linen runner with motifs worked by hand in silk threads

1935. Cobham Village WI. Surrey
Members of the Needlework Section of the Institute gained a Gold Star at the Redhill Handicraft Exhibition in 1935 for this cross stitched tablecover. The initials of the ladies who worked on the cloth were added in 1948. The cloth was cleaned by the Royal School of Needlwork in 2004. In 1935, when the cloth was made, there were 176 members of the Institute, with an average attendance of 120.
Cotton cross stitch on linen

1930. Merstham WI. Surrey
This cloth was made by twelve members of Merstham WI, under the leadership of Mrs Topham-Richardson, who may also have designed it.
Linen embroidered with wool threads

1938. Etchinghill WI. East Kent
The cloth shows Kent scenes and the county white horse emblem. Designed and made by Miss Shillingford.
Wool twill with hand stitched wool work panels

Newbold Pacey & Ashorne WI. Warwickshire
Linen with applied leather, velvet and crochet motifs

c.1940. Bearley WI. Warwickshire
Donated to the Institute by founder member Miss Doreen Deakin, and probably embroidered by her.
Pomegranates embroidered on linen with lace/crochet work insert and edgings

c.1956 Thornton Watlass WI. North Yorkshire
Proud members of Thornton Watlass and guests with their cloth, designed by Mrs Cowgill.
Cotton embroidery on linen

1951. Foxfield WI. Cumbria Westmorland
From their formation in 1934 the Foxfield WI had held their monthly meetings in a variety of venues including pubs, garages and members' houses. In February 1951 however, they opened their own, new, wooden building on land given by the local Lord of the Manor. Mrs Holiday made a new cloth to celebrate the occasion, using a transfer from Lancashire Federation for her design.
Felt appliqué with embroidery on green baize

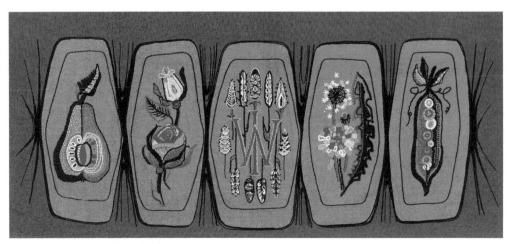

1968. Lymm Jubilee WI. Cheshire
This cloth, which was made for the formation of the Institute, was designed by Ann Mills and stitched by Mesdames Andrews, Barnes, Doxford and McLaren.
Linen fabric with applied linen panels hand embroidered using a variety of decorative stitches in soft cotton thread

c.1965. Broome WI. Worcestershire
Made by the Broome Sewing Guild.
Spring flowers in felt appliqué

c.1970. Painswick WI. Gloucestershire
This cover was made by members of the Institute to celebrate the Golden Jubilee of Painswick WI. It features the symbols of the hymn 'Jerusalem'.
Linen tablecloth embroidered appliquéd with stranded cotton and gold leather

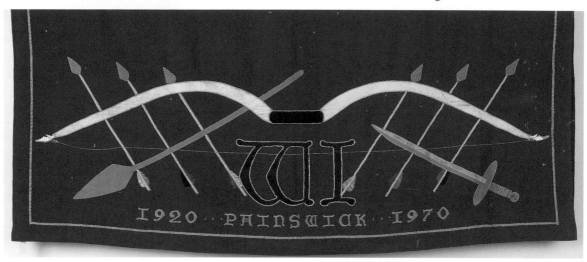

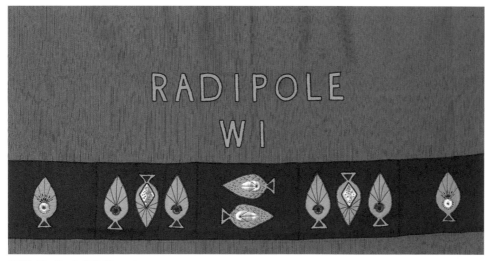

1970. Radipole WI. Dorset
This cover was made to commemorate the first Moon landing in 1969. Money was bequeathed by a member for the tablecover. Designed by Mrs. E.M. Gibbons and made by her with four other members.
Gold kid appliqué and embroidered felt shapes on cotton fabric

1982. Chellaston WI. Derbyshire
The frontal was made to celebrate the 50th anniversary of the Institute. It was designed by Chellaston's WI judge and tutor Margaret Mylrea, who was also on the DFWI Handicraft committee.
Gold kid appliqué and laid gold threads on dupion fabric

1985. (detail) Seaford Martello WI. East Sussex
The roundels on this cloth depict local landmarks and flowers.
Designed by members with Kathleen Amoore, and stitched by members under
the direction of Joyce Swinyard.
Cotton fabric with appliquéd roundels hand embroidered with stranded cotton

1993. Lockswood WI. Hampshire
28 members contributed to the making of
this cloth which was designed by Rosalind
Woodward with Phyllis Gurman. The
panels show garden flowers and the clock
tower, with the border featuring the
Hampshire Rose and local strawberries.
Mixed even-weave fabrics embroidered with
stranded cottons on twill background fabric

1993. Neatishead, Barton Turf and District WI. Norfolk
Made to celebrate the Institute's Diamond Jubilee, the
cloth was designed by Celia Scott, Drawn by Noel
Brandon Jones and made by 15 members.
Designs painted and over-stitched with stranded cottons on
linen background fabric

2000. Smallwood WI. Cheshire
Designed and made by Jean Batchelor to
celebrate the Millennium.
Appliqué with couched braids and some beading

Flower Design Cloths

Some techniques and styles have been consistently popular over the years. Flower patterns have been easily available as transfers or to copy from books, and the stitches used can be very simple or more complex according to the accomplishments of the maker. These cloths show the variety that can be achieved from a basic design feature and lots of colour.

1953. (detail) Great Barr. West Midlands
Made by members of the Institute.
Embroidery cottons on linen fabric with hand worked faggoting

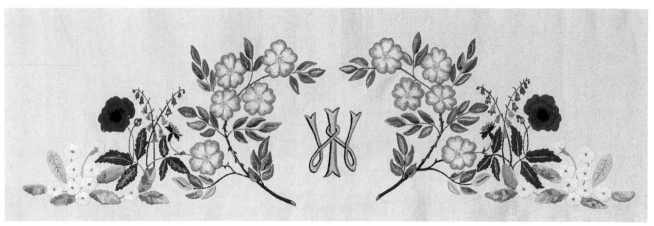

1957. Charing WI. East Kent
Designed by Mrs D. Hardwick and stitched by her and 8 other members of the Institute, the cloth was made for a Federation exhibition where it gained a Gold Star. The cloth was first used at the 36th birthday meeting of the Institute in June 1957.
Embroidery cottons on linen fabric

1953. Four Marks Afternoon WI. Hampshire
Wild and garden flowers.
Linen fabric with hand embroidery in stranded cotton

1993. North Kelsey WI. Lincolnshire North
Designed by Mrs Georgi Rawlins and embroidered by
members to celebrate the 60th anniversary of the Institute.
Embroidery cottons on cotton fabric. Knotted faggoting stitch
to join individually worked squares and edged with shell
design crochet

c.1965. Hook WI. East Yorkshire
Cotton embroidery on linen fabric with cotton crochet edging

c.1960. Ringway and Hale Barns WI. Cheshire
Linen, hand embroidered in stranded cotton

1955. Earls Barton WI. Northamptonshire
This cloth was started in 1953 by outgoing President
Mrs D.M. Richardson who embroidered the central motif.
Further members then embroidered the squares. It was
completed in two years.
Wool and cotton embroidery on a woollen cloth, lined with
muslin

1987. Word in Worth Evening WI. East Kent
Designed by Mrs Raynbird with Mrs Goldsack and made by several Institute members.
Cotton fabric with hand embroidery in a variety of stitches with padded appliqué fruit and vegetables

White and Lace-Edged Cloths

The simple white cloth and the elaborate lace or crochet lace border are both old favourites as a sure way to create a clean and luxurious-looking table. Some of these edgings have been worked to elaborate and unique patterns. Usually the cloths themselves are made of the finest materials but the recording project has identified several cloths made during war time from old flour or sugar sacks, lovingly embroidered, and they have proved very hard wearing.

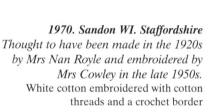

1970. Sandon WI. Staffordshire
Thought to have been made in the 1920s by Mrs Nan Royle and embroidered by Mrs Cowley in the late 1950s.
White cotton embroidered with cotton threads and a crochet border

1954. Moss Side Leyland WI. Lancashire
Made by Mrs Glover, Mrs Walmsley and Mrs Goode and used at the monthly meetings since 1954.
Cotton embroidery on cotton fabric with filet crochet edging

c.1960. Orwell WI. Cambridge
Designed and made by Mrs Bates.
Linen cloth with cotton crochet border

1974. Eastcote WI. Middlesex
Designed by Mrs Cuell and Mrs Hatcher and made by 5 members for the 50th anniversary of the Institute.
Linen embroidered with cotton, hand made lace edging

c.1940. (detail) Hartest & District WI. West Suffolk
This cloth was made out of two cotton flour sacks and still bears the lettering and numbers. Hand joined with a very fine seam, the cloth features the very popular crinoline lady motif.
Cotton sacking with hand embroidered motif

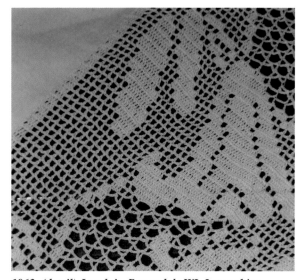

1963. (detail) Lumb-in-Rossendale WI. Lancashire
Made by Mrs M. Warburton with fabric and crochet lace donated by Mrs Blakeley, who probably worked the crochet border.
Cotton embroidery on linen cloth with crochet edging

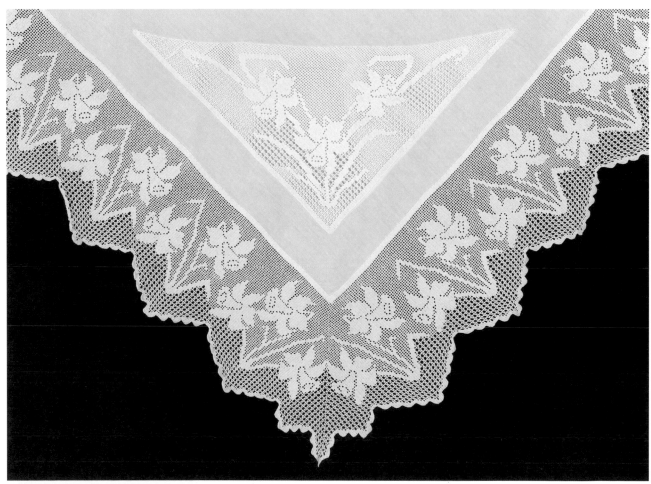

1979. Barnston WI. Cheshire
Made by Isobel Baxter and Enid Moreton as a birthday party cloth for the Institute.
Cotton cloth with cotton crochet edging and applied motifs

Signature Cloths

Getting people to sign textiles has long been a popular way of personalising a cloth or bedspread, and as a means of raising funds. There is a well-established tradition of churches and community organisations 'selling' table cloth or bedspread squares which were signed by the purchaser. The squares would then be made up and the completed item raffled off. Friendship and wedding quilts would be made up of signed squares and given as gifts. WI signature cloths usually record members' or the committee's names but some also record the names of visiting speakers. WI signature cloths are very common and many are an important historical record of members that sometimes are not recorded in any other form. Unfortunately, there is also a tendency to start inappropriately signing over very nice cloths that are not suited to this purpose. Most WI members would not dream of writing graffiti on walls, but some think nothing of ruining perfectly good cloths with ill spaced and illegible squiggles. Signature cloths should be well thought out from the start, worked evenly so they look acceptable at all stages of their development, and should only be worked on cloths designed for the purpose rather than appropriating a nicely worked old cloth that just isn't being used for anything else at the time. The following cloths illustrate various methods of working a signature cloth more successfully.

Badsey WI. Worcestershire
Made by Mrs Joyce Lashford for the Golden Jubilee of the Institute, the cloth has a ring of asparagus at the centre depicting a local industry, and the names of members in 1977.
Cotton cloth with cotton crochet edging

First Tower & Millbrook WI. Jersey
This cloth records all Presidents from 1951 to the present day as well as the Silver Jubilees of JFWI in 1975 and the Queen in 1977, together with the Golden Jubilees of NFWI in 1965, JFWI in 1999 and the Queen in 2003.
Cotton embroidery on linen fabric

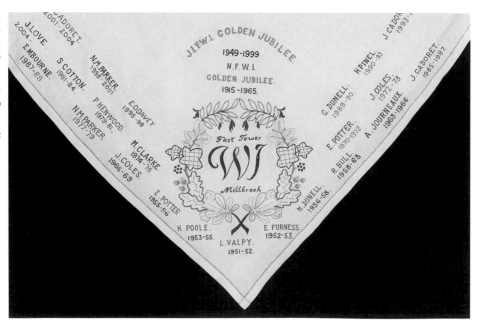

Corfe WI. Somerset
No records exist about the cloth, but the cloth itself records all the names and dates of the Presidents of Corfe WI. Probably made in 1935 (Institute founded in 1924).
Cotton embroidery on linen fabric

Killamarsh WI. Derbyshire
Possibly made in 1955, the cloth shows the names of all the officers of the Institute at the time of its formation in 1944 as well as members' signatures in the side panels.
Cotton embroidery on linen fabric

Askham Bryan WI. North Yorkshire East
This cloth, started in 1965, has the signatures of over 400 speakers and committee members between 1965 and 2006. Speakers include Alf Wright (James Herriot), Mrs Dench, Judi Dench's mother, and Sir Thomas Ingleby.
Stem stitch and chain stitch embroidery in cotton thread on linen fabric

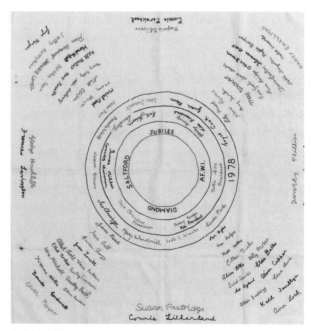

Saltford WI. Avon
Made in 1978 for the 60th anniversary of the Institute, the cloth records all the 1978 members.
Cotton embroidery on linen fabric

Gifts and Giving

Specially made textile items have been used as gifts for visitors and as 'thank you' presents to retiring officers by many WIs. Table covers and bedspreads have been very popular presents for retiring WI Presidents, and have usually been worked on by the full membership.

On a larger scale the West Kent bedspread was made up of contributions from every WI in the Federation. It was made for Mrs E.J. Heron Maxwell on her retirement as Chairman of the Federation in 1922. She had been elected as first Chairman of the new West Kent Federation in July 1918 and in that same year was elected to the NFWI Executive committee. She served from 1918 until 1926 and she was the first Chairman of the NFWI Handicraft sub-committee, playing a leading role in the development of WI handicraft nationally. She chaired the committee which organised the 1938 National Exhibition at The New Horticultural Halls, Westminster. Many years later the bedspread was returned to the Federation for safe-keeping.

Smaller items such as cushions and items of clothing have also been given as gifts. The slippers from Bitton WI were made by members in 1948 out of recycled parachute silk, lined and quilted, with soles made out of crocheted string. They are well-worn, so must have been much appreciated by retiring President Mrs. W.L. Smith. The slippers were returned to Bitton WI on her death.

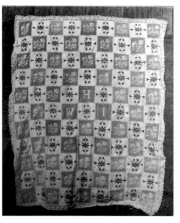

Bedspread. 1926 Headley WI. Hampshire
A gift from the Institute to their retiring President.

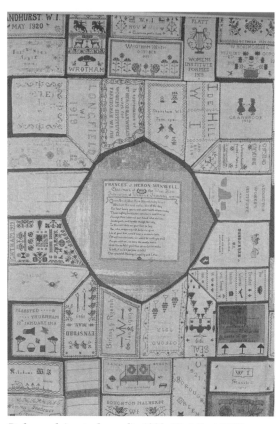

Bedspread (central panel). 1922. West Kent FWI
Separate shapes, individually worked and then joined together on a cotton base. Embroidered with cottons on linen fabric

Slippers. 1948. Bitton WI. Avon

Tablecover (detail). 1923. Wall WI. Staffordshire
This cloth appears to have been made by members of Wall WI and presented as a gift to their President Mrs Annie Ryman. Many years later, when Mrs Ryman's daughter passed away, the cloth was handed back to the Institute.
Linen embroidered with cotton. Individual panels joined with crochet

The gifts that have been most frequently recorded in 'Home and Country' are those given to various members of the royal family to celebrate special occasions, or when they have attended NFWI events.

'The Queen's Quilt' for Queen Mary was the idea of the NFWI Handicraft organiser Alice Armes. Each Federation asked members who wished to take part in making the quilt to submit examples of their work. Miss Armes went to the Federations to judge the squares for the Queen's Quilt and selected the three members from each county. The quilt measured 9ft by 8ft 8in. and the central panel was worked by members from East Sussex.

Embroidered bag. 1947. Shropshire FWI
This bag was made by Janet Barrow in 1947 and is recorded as being presented to Queen Mary on October 20th of that year. There is no record as to why the Federation still have the bag.
Linen with silk lining. Hand embroidered in silk

Queens Quilt 1929

In October 1929 the Queen who, in a tradition which continues today, was President of Sandringham WI, visited the NFWI Exhibition of Homecrafts at The Imperial Institute, where she was presented with the quilt. 'Home and Country' described the event:

"The visit of her Majesty the Queen gave great pleasure to the crowds of institute members who were fortunate to be there on that afternoon. The Queen who was received by the Chairman of the National Federation (Lady Denman) at the entrance, stopped to greet a fellow member from Norfolk. When Her Majesty regretted that she had forgotten to wear her institute badge the other Norfolk member was proud to pass on her badge which was worn by the President of Sandringham WI. Lady Denman on behalf of all the institutes in England and Wales presented Her Majesty with the bedspread of parchment coloured linen embroidered in yellow silk which for nine months has occupied the best needlewomen in every county. Her Majesty was charmed with the gift and said "It will go to Windsor for the yellow room".

Any member of the royal family visiting an exhibition or the WI stand at the Royal Show was presented with a gift and it was usually a piece of craft work. Gifts were also given to royalty as wedding presents. A table cloth was given to Princess Elizabeth on her wedding in 1947. The Queen Mother visited the WI exhibition in March 1960 at the Victoria and Albert Museum, and was presented with a ball for her new grandson who was then 25 days old. She was also presented with embroidered table cloths.

Many WIs have presented gifts to the Royal family but the majority of these are not recorded. There is no register of gifts to the Royal family between 1919 and 1952, and Buckingham Palace only has a record of two WI gifts to Queen Mary; a bedspread (1935) and a table cloth as a Wedding Gift. Three WI items are recorded as gifts to Queen Elizabeth the Queen Mother; an embroidered cushion from Rye WI (1979), an embroidered footstool from East Kent FWI (1979), and a lace handkerchief from St. Margaret's at Cliffe WI (1979). The following items were recorded as gifts to the Queen before 2004; lace handkerchieves from NFWI (1975), patchwork quilt from NFWI (1977), embroidered card from Nettlestone WI (1977), picture from Ipsley WI (1983), cushion from Hereford FWI (undated), goose nesting eggs from Thorncombe WI (undated).

The Textile Recording project has only recorded items belonging to WIs. By their very nature, gifts are given away, so they are not generally in the possession of the WI which made them. Items made as gifts are usually of the highest quality and have taken many hours to make. It is worth keeping a record of them by documenting and photographing them for the NNA before they are presented, in order to keep a record of the items for posterity.

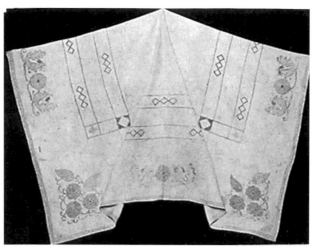

1947. Cloth made for the Wedding of Princess Elizabeth
The cloth was made by Mrs Emily Jane Dendy of Merrow Afternoon WI, Surrey. Later, Mrs Dendy made an exact replica of the cloth for her own daughter's wedding.

1960. The Queen Mother

Decoupage box. 2002. Haddiscoe & District WI, Norfolk
Copy of box card made by Jackie Woolsey for Queen Elizabeth on her Golden Jubilee.
Fabric covered hand made box with fabric decoupage on card

Federation Wall Hangings

Once Federations grew bigger they established headquarters as centres of county activities and organisation. During the late 20th century it became very popular to produce large collective wall hangings, made by all the Federation WIs, and which are still used as impressive features to decorate the walls of the headquarters buildings. These wall hangings have the same social function as banners in demonstrating the solidarity of the group, giving a sense of belonging to the figurehead organisation, and recording events and landmarks in the County. This type of group wall hanging is common in the wider community and many have been recorded by the NNA as part of The National Record of Millennium Needlework.

Wall Picture. 1989. Oxfordshire FWI
This is the centre panel of five wall hangings made to commemorate the 70th anniversary of the Federation. It was designed by Brenda Poulter of Harwell WI, and made by members of Stoke Lyne WI.
Silver kid appliqué on wool canvas work

Wall Hanging. 1999. Teesside FWI
This Millennium wall hanging was designed by college lecturer Fiona Thompson and made by 12 WI members with students from Cleveland College of Art and Design. The group received a grant from 'Arts for All' to make the work. Landmarks depicted include:
Guisborough Priory, Roseberry Topping, St. Mary's Cathedral, Tees Barrage, Bottle of Notes (Middlesborough), Yarm Viaduct, Transporter Bridge, Capt. Cook's ship Endeavour, Zetland – the oldest lifeboat in G.B., Cooling towers at Hartlepool Power Station, I.C.I. works and Darlington Brick Train.
Made in ten sections on calico backing with mixed fabrics and embroidery

Generally, these communal wall hangings take two distinct forms; – the 'album' style collective, which consists of many individually embroidered rectangles, stitched together, such as those from Humberside and Tyneside Federations; – and the mural collage, where many small embroidered features are applied on to a background fabric, which may be painted or embroidered. Staffordshire, Teesside and Essex Federations all have examples of this type of work. Of course, wall hangings may combine these styles in various ways, either in the same piece, or in picture sets. The panel from Oxfordshire Federation, for instance, is the centre piece of a group of five wall hangings, the outer ones being album collectives.

Wall Panels. 1982. Essex FWI
These panels were designed by Margaret Abbess for the Committee Room at the Essex Federation Headquarters.
The panels depict events in WI history and activities in the Essex Federation.
Varied embroidery techniques on linen. Mounted on board

Wall Hanging. 1989. Tyneside FWI
Squares made by Institutes, and the hanging made up by Margaret Clementson to celebrate the
10th anniversary of the Federation.
Mixed techniques on calico

Wall Hanging/Table Frontal. 1999. Staffordshire FWI
This dual purpose work was designed by Mrs Anita Murphy and worked by members of the Arts
and Crafts Sub-Committee to celebrate the 80th anniversary of the Federation.
Appliquéd buildings on a painted calico ground fabric, in the shape of a Staffordshire knot

Wall Hanging. 1996. Humberside FWI
The hanging shows the WIs in the Federation in 1996.
Embroidered on calico, set into cotton sashings and borders

1921. Lace makers at Catforth WI. Lancashire

Industry

WI shop Warwick. 1923

The first WIs in Britain, formed in 1915 and 1916, were under the auspices of the Agricultural Organisation Society (AOS). The AOS had been set up in 1901 to offset the serious agricultural decline and help to prevent the drift of workers from the land to the cities that had been taking place in the latter part of the nineteenth century. The AOS started local societies of farmers, small holders and growers so that they could work co-operatively to improve their output. Although it had been suggested that the AOS might inaugurate a purely women's organisation on the Canadian Women's Institutes model, the Society showed no interest until John Nugent Harris, the Secretary of AOS, met Madge Watt who was visiting Britain from Canada and keen to get WIs started. The AOS employed her in 1915 and she formed the first WI at Llanfair PG on Anglesey. The aims of these first WIs were to increase food supply, develop village industries and prepare for reconstruction.

With the AOS's commitment to trading, the WIs were seen as a means of providing work for the women of rural communities thus offering a chance to earn some money and help the rural economy during wartime. The first minutes of the AOS WI sub-committee of Dec 2nd 1915 agreed "That as far as possible some form of co-operative effort suitable to the district, should be put before each institute from the outset." The majority of the crafts that were traded were textile based.

The minutes of the meeting of AOS WI sub-committee on 3rd July 1917 recorded that:

"Mrs Whitaker, who has occasionally lectured to different WIs on Labour Saving Devices, attended the committee to report on a toy development in Sussex. A topical toy rabbit 'Cuthbert' has attracted the attention of the trade. After discussion it was felt there is a possibility of the WIs starting a WI village toy industry."

The majority of the toys involved, including 'Cuthbert', were soft toys made from fabric. With all commercial manufacturing at this time turned away from 'luxury' products, and with no imports, these toys were extremely popular.

c.1918
Sussex Cuthberts and other toys.

By the time the responsibility for WIs was handed over to the Board of Agriculture in 1917, many of these village industries had started, or were planned. Once the NFWI was formed in 1918, an advisory Trades sub-committee was created (later the Industries sub-committee) to oversee toy making and marketing. After visiting the Sussex Toy Scheme, which was where 'Cuthbert' had originated, they advocated the formation of a limited company for the central organisation of toy making in the WIs. The Women's Institute Toy Society was registered as a Trading Society in July 1918 and an 'Industries lecturer' was appointed as a travelling officer to deal with village industries. Teachers were appointed and small loans were available to WIs for materials. Later, other crafts and fruit preservation were included in the industry brief. However, by 1919 with the end of the war, and with transport, marketing and quality issues, the initiative floundered and in June 1919 the Toy Society trading arm was wound up. Despite this, toy making has continued to be a very successful craft within the WI throughout its history. Specialist tutors and judges have been trained and courses run at local and national level. This expertise has frequently been used by outside bodies. Mrs Gwynneth Lord, toy tutor and judge, of Packington and Maxstoke WI, Warwickshire, twice appeared on the 'Generation Game' TV show demonstrating how to stuff soft toys, including a toy camel. Toys have also reflected regional influences such as the Hereford bull from Herefordshire, and the doll from Guernsey.

Banner. 1936. Bridport Centre WI. Dorset
Many banners have designs which reflect their local industries. Making nets in Dorset was a cottage industry involving many women.
Appliqué on Bridport sailcloth

Herefordshire Bull
Kept in the Herefordshire Room at Denman College.

Easter Rabbit
Made by Mrs Gwynneth Lord of Packington and Maxstoke WI, Warwickshire.

Doll. Guernsey FWI
Kept in the Guernsey Federation Room at Denman College, the doll is wearing a sun bonnet.

In 1919 it was clear from the experience of the Toy Industry that the way forward was not in a centrally organised industry. However this was not the end of the story because ventures did continue but were organised on local lines. In some areas of the country members had been making money through selling craft work locally for some time. For example the Essex Federation, formed in September 1917, had a market stall sub-committee. A section of their market stall was devoted to handicrafts of every kind, including soft toys and plain needlework. Toy Society papers record: "A halfpenny commission is charged on all goods sold, and in less than four months £300 has gone directly into the pockets of members." Lindfield WI, Sussex, produced 1,900 toys during one year with one member making £20 'pocket money' as the result of her share in the industry.

Throughout the 1920s and 1930s there were a number of very successful local 'cottage industries'. Some of these sold their work co-operatively through shops set up by the local Federation although they all had a problem with maintaining the quality of workmanship.

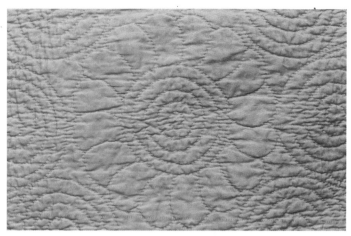

Quilt segment (detail). 1950. Durham FWI
WIs made items for sale using local traditional crafts. Durham quilt making was a well established cottage industry. This segment is part of one of three quilts made by Mrs Black and Mrs Lough for the Durham Federation room at Denman College. The quilts were in place until 1999, and this segment was retained.
Durham quilting on cotton fabric

Gloves. 1940s.
Suffolk West FWI
Example of 'Thrift' gloves.
Presented to SWFWI by Miss Flack.
Grey flannel embroidered with black wool

c.1930
Hampshire WI shop Winchester.

Table Cover. 1978. Steeple Ashton WI. Wiltshire
Designed by Mrs M Haythornewaite and stitched by members of Steeple Ashton WI, the cloth depicts the wool trade for which the village was famous in the Middle Ages.
Woollen fabric with appliqué and embroidery stitches

Country-wide, WIs and Federations also continued to trade in old crafts which were well established, such as wool related crafts, quilting in Durham and smock-making in several country areas. Ticehurst WI, Sussex, was notable for smocking under the leadership of Lady Julian Parr, herself a gifted craftswoman who had gained a first prize in the National Exhibition of 1919. They continued to make smocked children's dresses, which were advertised in *The Lady*, and sold through *Liberty's*, until the late 1930s.

Child's Smocked Dress. 1925. NFWI
Made by Miss A. Quinton, Hayes WI. Kent.
Green cotton fabric with traditional smocking stitches in cotton threads

Child's Smocked Dress. NFWI
Probably made as a tutor's sample or competition piece.
Blue chambray fabric with cotton threads. Traditional smocking stitches

Child's Smocked Dress. c.1958. Penally WI. Pembrokeshire
Made for a WI competition by several members of Penally WI including Molly Whitehead and Nan Jones.
Welsh wool embroidered and smocked with cotton threads

Cushion Cover. c.1955. NFWI
Smocking patterns on linen

Adult's Smock. c.1925. NFWI
A Staffordshire gardener's smock. Part of the Alice Armes NFWI collection of smocks relating to her book 'English Smocks' pub.1926. Miss Armes was an NFWI Craft Adviser.
Linen with smocking to back and front of bodice, sleeves and collar

Smock Pattern Sampler. c.1955. NFWI
Made by Mrs Harmer of East Kent Federation
Blue cotton fabric with white cotton stitching

Following the First World War, the view of craft within the NFWI had changed from industry to a maintenance of quality, and preservation of tradition. In addition, with the return to the country of male workers after the war, a major consideration was that the women WI members were not working for below the standard rate of pay in competition with men. Government wished to discourage women from paid work now the war was over and by 1920 WI craft was seen as a 'useful activity' rather than a means of income. In spite of this there were many WIs where industries did still flourish. There are frequent references in 'Home and Country' to these throughout the 1920s and 1930s. In 1921, Hyde Heath WI, Buckinghamshire, reported in 'Home and Country' the revival of an old industry where the WI "has started straw splitting and plaiting which for many years was one of the rural industries in Buckinghamshire, also Buckinghamshire lace making."

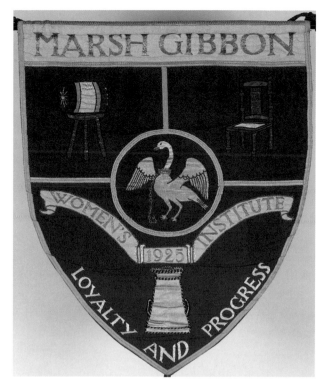

Banner. 1925. Marsh Gibbon WI. Buckinghamshire
The banner shows a Buckingham wooden chair, a lace maker's cushion and a milk churn around a chained Buckinghamshire swan. This design was the winning entry in a competition for Marsh Gibbon WI members. Mrs. Simms, the wife of the village wheelwright and herself a lace maker, won 5/- for her design. There is no record of who made the banner although it may well have been Mrs Simms herself. Lace making was a prominent home industry with a lace making school recorded in the village in 1858.
Linen with appliqué and gold silk embroidery with applied braids

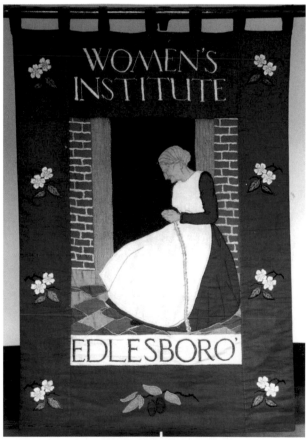

Banner. 1934. Edlesborough WI. Buckinghamshire
This banner shows straw plait making and plum blossom indicating the two main Edlesborough industries in which women were involved in 1934. The plums were primarily used for dye making. Edlesborough WI banner can be seen on parade in 1947 on page 20.
Cotton with embroidery on appliqué. Straw plait

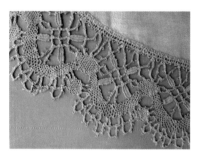

Lace Mat (detail). Wells next the Sea WI. Norfolk
Made by Mrs Stringer as an exact copy of a design by her Great Grandmother and donated to the Institute.
Linen centre with Bedford cotton lace edging

Paperweight. c.1992. Hertfordshire FWI
Kept in the Hertfordshire Federation Room at Denman College.
Cotton Lace

In 1925 'Home and Country' noted that the Knitting Industry in Piddlehinton WI, Dorset, had over forty members and in six months twenty pairs of short stockings and thirty seven pairs of socks were sold.

During the economic depression of the 1930s women's earnings were valuable additions to a family's income and cross stitch work was a suitable cottage industry technique. In Twyford, Hampshire, Miss Louisa Pesel established the Yew Tree Industry to help the women whose husbands were out of work. The women made cross stitch items of many kinds which were sold at high class London shops. Although not a WI Industry directly, many of the women were WI members and the WI continued to do the embroidery even after the organised work finished. It is thought that some of the members who made the cloth for Twyford WI had been workers for the Yew Tree initiative.

Textile crafts again took on a commercial aspect for WIs during the Second World War when women were once more encouraged to work and earn. The development of the regular WI market stalls was a good outlet for many items which had again become unobtainable from large manufacturers or from overseas.

Table Cover (detail). 1950. Twyford WI. Hampshire
Designed by Etta Campbell who taught at the Winchester
School of Art, and made by WI members.
Linen embroidered with cotton threads

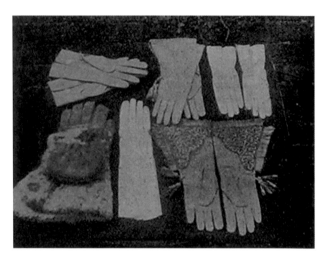

1922
Gloves on sale from Dunchurch WI.

1925
Piddlehinton WI Knitting Industry Group.

A development of the embroidery on the centre panel of the traditional smock led to the very popular Dorset Feather stitch. Mrs Olivia Pass, then Chairman of the Dorset Federation's Craft sub-committee combined old patterns with her knowledge of Eastern European decorative stitches to create a technique which was easy to work and very effective in its style. Mrs Pass started to teach this technique for students to use both for pleasure and profit. In 1951 Mrs Pass and her original eighty students put on a very successful sale of Dorset Feather stitched work at the Bath and West Agricultural Show. The technique was immediately popular and in 1957 Mrs Pass published her book 'Dorset Feather Stitchery'. This book has been in print almost continually ever since, with its ninth edition published in 1997 by the Dorset Federation. Not limited to Dorset, the technique was quickly adopted all over the country.

Apron worked with Dorset Feather Stitch Embroidery

Book Cover. 1990. Colehill Evening WI. Dorset
Made by Miss May Lisher and other members of the Institute for their 25th anniversary.
Linen embroidered with cotton threads

Table Cover. c.1966. Sidford WI. Devon
Made by Mavis Wotton, President Sidford WI 1965-66.
Dorset feather stitching on linen with tatting edge

Table Cover. 1960. West Dean WI. West Sussex
This cloth was first proposed in 1958 with all members adding at least a few stitches over the following two years.
Linen with Dorset feather stitched borders

Table Cover. c. 1980. Middlewood & Higher Poynton WI. Cheshire
Made by Marjorie Huxley.
Linen embroidered with stranded embroidery threads

Other Federations too developed their own designs for textiles. The 'Middlesex' design represents the River Thames, the traffic on the river, bridges and green belt acorns. One rule is *not* to use Dorset Feather stitch patterns on a 'Middlesex' design!

In 1977, in response to the Prince of Wales's appeal for the Queen's Silver Jubilee, the NFWI agreed with Debenham's store in Oxford Street to take over a department within the shop to sell craft work made by WI members. The money raised would go the appeal. WI members responded with vast amounts of craft work, so much so that the store was quite overwhelmed. A letter came from Buckingham Palace thanking the NFWI for "The magnificent first donation of £25,000 from some hundred thousand items that poured into London from every part of the country"

In 1995 the markets arm of the NFWI split away, on the recommendation of the Charity Commission and NFWI's legal advisers, to form 'WI Country Markets', and in 2004 the WI was dropped from the name. This is now a separate commercial organisation which is very successful, trading locally-produced goods at markets and village halls.

Table Cover. 1964. Harlington WI. Middlesex
The 'Middlesex' design made by Harlington WI members.
Cotton fabric and braids, embroidered with cotton threads

1977
NFWI craft items offered for sale at Debenham's Oxford Street store.

Wall hanging. 1935. South Baddesley WI. Hampshire
The picture was made in 1935 by Amy and Jean Waldie. It was mounted on the green linen background fabric in 1961 and displayed at the County Exhibition of wall hangings. The picture depicts a market scene, possibly WI stalls.
Appliqué and embroidery on linen fabric

Education

The first constitution of the NFWI, adopted in 1917, gave the main purpose of the National Federation as

"to provide an organisation with the object of enabling women to take an effective part in rural life and development."

It undertook to do this by providing:

"for the fuller education of countrywomen in citizenship, in public questions both national and international, in music, drama and other cultural subjects and also to secure instruction and training in all branches of agriculture, handicrafts, domestic science, health and social welfare."

The failure of the Industries initiative of the early years was followed by a determination on the part of the NFWI to concentrate on education. In December 1919 the Industries sub-committee reported to the NFWI Executive committee that they proposed a change in policy regarding handicraft work:

"In accordance with the resolution passed at the AGM the sub-committee proposed working towards a revival of handicraft for home use rather than the development of trade industries."

They proposed setting up a Guild of Learners to improve rural life and encourage home handicrafts. Subsequently the Handicraft sub-committee agreed that:

"the system of loans for trading be abolished....that the existing fund be used for craft educational purposes."

'Co-operative' in WI terms was now to be interpreted as 'working together' and not as a trading concern.

The 'Guild of Learners of Home Craft' was launched in February 1920 at a conference of County Handicraft Organisers in London. At the following Consultative Council Miss Preece, the Handicraft Technical Organiser, put on a small exhibition of crafts to promote the Guild.

Embroidered Purse. Mrs A.H. Christie
This purse was illustrated in the magazine 'Embroidery' in January 1909. A pattern was offered to readers.
Needlepoint in silks with corded bindings and handle

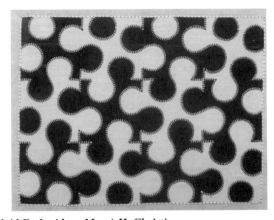

Inlaid Embroidery, Mrs A.H. Christie
Inlay appliqué worked in linen

Sampler. 'The Quarrel' Mrs A.H. Christie
Mrs Christie was a teacher of embroidery and published several books. The two samplers above were made for the book 'Samplers and Stitches' first published in 1934. They were given to the NFWI and are now at Denman College.

A leaflet printed and distributed in the 1920s described the Guild of Learners purpose as restoring the best traditions of English workmanship and promoting the best instruction within the reach of villages. It went on to outline the certificates and craft schools available which included weaving, spinning, dressmaking and tailoring, leather, upholstery, lace making, knitting, crochet, dyeing, straw plaiting, plain or decorated needlework, skin curing and mounting, toy making, glove making, and rug making. A series of proficiency tests were gradually introduced which a member had to complete before she could train as a demonstrator, instructor or judge. The first test was held in September 1920 and it was for glove making.

The first national course to be organised by the Handicraft sub-committee was a five day course in September 1920 at The Victoria and Albert Museum. The subject was 'Decorative Stitchery' and included lectures, visits to exhibits, and to the library. Course topics were *The History of Ornament* – Professor Newberry, *Chinese symbolism*, *Dress embroidery for present time* – Miss Drew, *Embroideries seen in Czecho-Slovakia* – Miss Drew, *Banners* – Commander Kettlewell, and *Handwork as the basis of civilisation* – Miss Preece. This is a syllabus that would be equally popular today.

The Guild of Learners' first priority was to train and appoint leaders who would become the teachers, trainers and demonstrators for the WI members throughout the country. In November 1920 the first 'school' to be organised outside London was held at the Technical Institute in Tunbridge Wells. This school was followed by similar ones in Malvern and in Leeds. With a pool of members trained, in 1921 Area Organisers began to be appointed to teach, inspect and judge handicrafts. The second proficiency tests were organised in glove making, decorative stitching, basket work and rush work. The third proficiency tests took place the following year and included upholstery and lace making.

Guild of Learners badge. Mrs Charlton

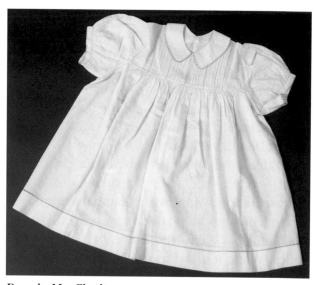
Dress by Mrs Charlton
Fine Cotton

Sewing Samples
Made by Mrs Charlton for her Guild of Learners badge in the 1940s.
Hand sewing and embroidery on cotton

'Home and Country' carried a regular column and articles on Needlework. In 1922 there was a series of articles, 'Hints on Embroidery', written by Joan Drew, and the first paper patterns were introduced that could be ordered from the magazine.

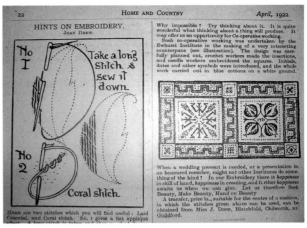

1923. 'Home and Country' article

The Area Schools continued teaching leather gloving, embroidery, soft toys, plain sewing, and millinery, and new proficiency tests were added in smocking and leather design. Many WI-trained teachers started to work for the local authorities and there was a demand for more WI teachers. Local classes tended to be in practical subjects such as dressmaking and millinery.

The Guild of Learners also created a Loan Collection, which was a collection of items of different crafts, all packed into a basket or box which could be easily transported, and which could be borrowed by Federations. Items were selected to show excellence in each craft. It was built up gradually, some items were acquired especially, and some, as reported in 'Home and Country' were donated:

"Miss Drew has presented the collection with two specimens of her own work – a child's frock with seam decorations, and a tray cloth in black on cream where the hem is treated very suggestively".

Needle Case. 1990. Buckinghamshire FWI
Made for the Buckinghamshire Loan Collection.
Drawn fabric techniques worked on linen

The National loan collections were enlarged and kept up to date and Federations also put together their own loan collections. Many Federations still maintain a loan collection but the National collection has been disbanded.

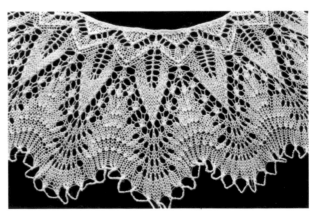

Knitted Lace Collar 1982. Buckinghamshire FWI
The collar was knitted from a commercial pattern for the Buckinghamshire Loan Collection.
Fine wool

During the Second World War, with materials in short supply, handicraft work concentrated on 'make do and mend' and the NFWI published a very popular booklet on thrift crafts which included making outfits and furnishings out of scraps or remodelled clothes. Once the war was over the emphasis reverted once more to teaching and raising standards. In 1948 NFWI circulated a 'Questionary' to County Handicraft Committees asking about the classes they had run. In the analysis of these returns the following came out in order of popularity: Dressmaking, Leather work, Basketry, Rugs, Gloves, Soft toys, Upholstery, Quilting, Embroidery.

Denman College was opened in 1948 in response to the perceived need for a People's College of Adult Education. Courses were offered in a variety of subjects, many of them textile related. In the 1950s the popular 'Country Housewife' courses included some craft work, but there were also specialist subjects such as:

1951 Upholstery, linen embroidery, the making of underclothes

1952 Upholstery, soft furnishing, smocking, gloving, fabric printing, cross-stitch

1955 Loose covers, lampshades, re-covering eiderdowns, machine knitting, tatting

1956 Sewing new fabrics, tailoring.

In the 1950s the 'Guild of Learners of Handicrafts' changed its name to 'The Handicraft Guild', but they continued to administer the proficiency tests. The list of crafts now included clothes renovation, machine work, mending and upholstery.

c.1930 Upholstery Class

Plain Sewing Class in Wartime

Teaching Aid Sample Books. 1950s and 1960s. Warwickshire FWI
A set of display board teaching samples for use at classes.
Various fabrics and techniques, mounted on board

In 1966 correspondence courses were started by NFWI as a way of helping WI members to learn a new craft if they were not able to find a local class. The first of these were: canvas work, patchwork, basketry and embroidery. The work could be sent to a tutor for comment and advice. Various craft advisers over the years had commented on the importance of design in craft work and finally in 1967 a new Design Award was announced, for work having special merit by showing all round high standard of design, to start in 1968.

A major reorganisation took place in 1972. The Handicraft Guild was abolished (along with the Produce Guild) and was replaced by the Home Economics department. There was some resistance to this and certainly in some Federations a craft committee was retained, at least for some time, so that the crafts aspect maintained its high profile.

In 1977 Home Economics Basic Certificates replaced proficiency tests. A modern syllabus was produced and the candidates had to submit for examination not only the required craft items but also 'working notebooks'. In 1978, 252 certificates were awarded and the Design Award was given to 7 members from 39 entries.

WI members received help and advice about various crafts through articles, first in 'The Landswoman' and then in 'Home and Country'. Once NFWI was established, the publications department began to produce small leaflets, costing only a few pence, on a whole range of crafts. It was not until 1977, with the formation of WI Books Ltd., that a new era of publishing began. Hardback books, rather than pamphlets, were produced and aimed at the general public as well as WI members, with the aim not only of education, but also of making a profit for the NFWI.

Sampler. 1956. Bashley WI. Hampshire
This whitework sampler was made by Mrs Maude Croft and entered in a competition with 'Woman's Journal'. It came 6th out of 73 entries. Mrs Croft gave the sampler to the Institute and it was rediscovered amongst old record books in 1997, when it was reframed.
Whitework stitches on cotton

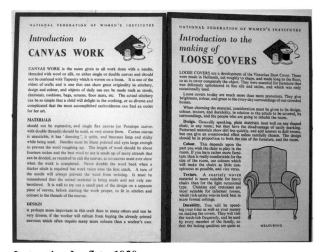

Instruction Leaflets. 1950s

Booklet. 1979. Quilting

Booklet. 1975. Soft Toys

In the late 1970s, as grants from the Government were reduced, NFWI began to make links with commercial sponsors. In 1979 the Design award was run in association with the British Wool Marketing Board. The East Sussex member who won was able to see her design modelled on the cat walk at a fashion show. In 1984 the Award was reviewed again and it was decided to broaden its scope and subsequently it has been used for non craft subjects as well, for example exhibition and garden design.

In the 1990s 'Action Packs' were developed. Devised by specialist craft advisers these packs enabled a group to learn a skill without a tutor, following step by step instructions. Travelling tutors provided another way in which WIs could get tuition in some of the more specialist crafts where they might not find a class locally.

In the 1990s there was also a policy of seeking external accreditation for the qualifications offered through the NFWI. Accreditation was sought through the Open College Network, which also enables Denman College to access funding via a franchise with Abingdon College. In craft work in particular, NFWI built up a relationship with City and Guilds. As with the qualifications through the Guild of Learners in the 1920s and 1930s, it is only a small number of people who take these advanced qualifications, but those who do are important as they become the teachers of the future.

Design Award. 1979

Tatting Samples. 1980s. Derbyshire FWI
Stella Haywood's collection of tatting samples are used for exhibition and as teaching aids.

Patchwork Quilt. 2003. NFWI
Made for the Chairman's room at Denman College by Mrs Pat Lumsdale.
Cotton fabrics with applied designs

Home ......

Women's Work!

From the earliest days of the WI, one of the highest priorities was improvement in the home. This involved the sharing of expertise from neighbours as well as more formal education and training in household skills. In April 1919 the NFWI appointed Miss Preece as Technical Organiser. Her brief was to ensure adequate standards of handicraft work. Miss Preece was influenced by the Arts and Crafts movement and was keen to see the WI reviving traditional rural crafts. In February 1920, in *Notes on Handicraft*, a column she wrote for 'Home and Country', she reported on a conference of Educational Associations where reference was made to the WI movement:

"It was said in connection with 'Home making as a basis of citizenship' that a great loss had come to the home through the habit of supplying needs with the ready-made, that when (as in our grandmothers' time) women provided the family with food, clothing and even medicines from their own knowledge, they took a more active part in the production of raw materials for these purposes and thus found greater interest in their work.....in order to regain the true home-making spirit (which at present is almost unknown) it is necessary to recover those lost arts within the home which give pleasure in the doing and secure lasting satisfaction. On the practice of these arts rests the basis of good citizenship."

The working of textiles both for practical and decorative purposes was necessarily at the forefront of this drive for women to again take pride in being at home.

Work Box. 1984. Berkshire FWI
Designed and made by Janet Clark for the Berkshire Room at Denman College. The ladies on the box are doing household jobs and the text around the box says "Women's Work is Never Done".
Stumpwork figures with cross stitch lettering on linen

Banner. 1954. Wolvercote WI. Oxfordshire
This banner is a copy of an older, very worn, banner. It was made by Mesdames Hutchins, England, Stay, Spickernell and Slaughter, using money collected for a memorial to a past President, Miss Morris Smith.
Felt with wool embroidery

Quilts and bedspreads for the home were usually very decorative, but even kitchen items such as the tea cosy embroidered by Mrs Jenkins in 1929 have been wonderfully worked. Another kitchen item designed by many WIs is the common tea towel. Although thousands of these have probably been produced by WIs with pictures of themselves, their locality, or certain events, only three were recorded by WIs across the whole country. Some WIs may have recorded their designs and dates in year books, but the majority seem to have kept no trace.

Rug making was a good home craft for recycling old clothes and for giving a bright new look to a room. It is a craft that has become popular again in recent years.

Tea Towel. 1999. Morley WI. Derbyshire
Designed by Geoffrey S. Toms and commercially printed, this Tea towel depicts village landmarks. Produced to celebrate 50 years of the Institute, 350 were printed and are known to have been sent to several countries around the world.
Screen printed cotton

Tea Cosy. 1929. NFWI
Made by Mrs Jenkins for the 1929 NFWI Exhibition. Queen Mary remarked on the beauty of the work and it gained marks of 98%.
Silk embroidery on linen

1938 WI rugs at an exhibition

Banner. 1995. Wolviston Village WI. Teesside
Worked by several members of the Institute using recycled materials.
Hooked rug on hessian backing

Banner. 1940. Great Barton. West Suffolk
Bertuna, the Gleaner, is the village emblem as Great Barton held the grain store for the Abbey in Bury St. Edmunds.
Figure worked in petit-point, lettering worked in silk, both appliquéd on to linen fabric

Boxes

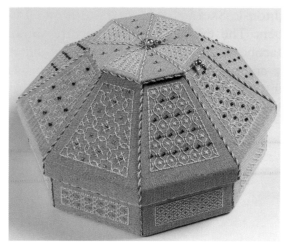

Willoughby WI. Warwickshire
Designed and made by Mrs H. Martin, an artist and embroidery tutor.
Blackwork techniques and beading on linen

c.1982. Shropshire FWI
Designed and made by Kath Harper.
Satin moiré with hand worked beaded decoration

c.1982. Shropshire FWI
Set of boxes designed and made by Kath Harper.

1990. Buckinghamshire FWI
Made for the Buckinghamshire Federation's Loan Collection.
Drawn Fabric work on linen

1983. Buckinghamshire FWI
Designed and made by Barbara Hirst of Seer Green and Jordans WI who won the NFWI Design Award in 1983.
Padded calico with needlelace, couching and french knots

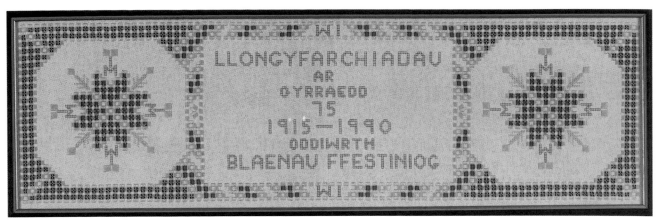

Birthday Card. 1990. Blaenau Ffestiniog WI. Gwynedd Merionnydd
Made by Nancy Evans to celebrate the 75th Birthday of the NFWI.
'Congratulations on Reaching 75. 1915-1990 from Blaenau Ffestiniog WI'.
Hardanger on cotton evenweave fabric

Tray cloth. c.1993. Hertfordshire FWI
Used in the Hertfordshire Room at Denman College.
Linen with drawn thread work

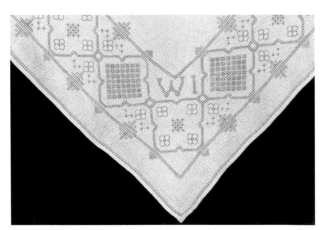

Table Cover. 1950s. Cottenham WI. Cambridgeshire
Made by Mrs. Cliff Furbank.
Drawn thread work on evenweave linen

Book Cover. 1954. Rowlands Castle WI. Hampshire
This is the cover of the first scrapbook of Rowlands Castle
WI which was formed in 1946. It was designed by Edith
Clarke and all members stitched some part of it.
Linen with cross stitch and drawn thread work

Table Cover. 1988. Alverstone WI. Isle of Wight
Worked by several members of this WI from
patterns in a Hardanger book.
Hardanger technique in self coloured threads on
cream evenweave cotton

Community

On the wider plane of life in the village, WIs were encouraged to play an active part in the community in an organised way, thus making a greater impact than individuals alone. Lady Denman's 1918 message to WIs, published in 'The Landswoman', stressed how important she felt the role of WIs should be in the community:

"The Ideal: that every member is an energetic and thinking participant in the life of the Women's Institute, and through the Institute, in the life of the village."

During the 1920s and 30s 'Home and Country' reported on the many ways in which WIs were using their craft skills to help the community. There were concerns about children having to walk to school in all weathers and so in 1925 some WIs "…made slippers for school children out of old felt hats ….were much appreciated by scholars and parents alike."

Shoes from felt hats and old deck chairs were also made during the Second World War.

The district nurse was a valued member of the community and in pre National Health Service days WI members were keen to support the local nurse and hospital. WIs reported such help as providing a maternity bag or a layette for the nurse to give to a needy family, and making emergency bags for any man or woman who did not have the necessary outfit if they had to go into the Infirmary. WIs also provided knitted bed socks, flannel bed jackets, towels, and pillowcases for local cottage hospitals. Some WIs provided screens for their village halls which were used for health services such as child welfare and chiropody clinics. While the majority of these screens were plain fabrics on metal frames, some of the earlier ones were very elaborately decorated.

1940s. Shoes made from felt hats and deck chairs

Screen. c.1934. Albury Evening WI. Surrey
This screen was worked by 36 members of Albury WI to a design by Miss Joan Drew. The subjects are 'old happenings in Albury'. The screen was exhibited at the NFWI exhibition at the Horticultural Hall in 1935 and was awarded a Gold Star.
Linen embroidered in fine wool

THE·OLD·CHURCH A·D 1000
REJOICINGS
IN·1815

Framed segment of curtain. 1959.
Kennington WI. East Kent
This is one of the remaining fragments from
the 18 village hall curtains embroidered by
members of Kennington WI. There were
6 panels to each curtain, making 108 panels
in total. When the curtains were replaced in
1979 two other pieces were used to cover WI
scrapbooks.
Linen fabric embroidered with stranded cottons

Curtain. c.1925. West Kent FWI
One of a remaining set of three,
the curtains were possibly made
by Mrs J. Pearson of Seal WI.
Embroidered in wool on natural
coloured linen

Pair of Curtains. 1927. Sutton Green WI. Surrey
Early in their life these village hall curtains were
shown at an NFWI Exhibition in London and
were awarded a Gold Star. Made by
19 members of Sutton Green WI, they have
been in constant use ever since.
Heavy linen fabric with appliqué in silk, and
embroidered with wool and silk threads

From the end of the war in 1918, villages tried to rebuild their communities and great value was put on local activities and social life. Many villages acquired new, or extended their existing, village halls, and many WIs bought their own halls. WI members played their part in equipping these halls; reports included making curtains both for the windows and the stage. This support for village halls has continued through the decades and, in textiles, has included wall hangings, table covers and cushions for chairs.

Providing toys for sick or disadvantaged children has been regular community work for the WI. In 1926 Potters Bar WI, Hertfordshire, made 576 toys to send to children in hospital. A photograph of them appeared in 'Home and Country'.

In Cheshire in 1927 several WIs dressed dolls which were given either to poor children in Manchester or to children's hospitals. In the Golden Jubilee year of 1965 there was a national initiative to produce toys. 'Home and Country' reported that at 'The Countrywoman Today' exhibition at the Ceylon Tea Centre: "An enormous number of toys were on display – made by members for distribution to hospitals and handicapped children."

Banner. 1989. Wombourne WI. Staffordshire
This banner was made to parade at the celebrations for the 70th anniversary of this WI. The building depicted is the WI hall, Wombourne. The banner was stitched by Mrs Rock and Mrs Fisher, with help on the design from Mrs Griffiths.
Felt, with appliqué and embroidery stitches

1926. Toys for hospitalised children

c.1956. Making curtains

Fox Doll. c.1965
Sample doll for community projects made by Gwynneth Lord, WI Soft Toy Tutor and Judge.

The village parish church has also gained from the skill of WI craft workers and there are many reports of help in making church furnishings. One of the most ambitious must be the altar frontal made by WI members for York Minster, but many parish churches have kneelers made by WI members. The NNA keeps a record of kneeler projects and designs as one of its national recording programmes, but as the kneelers no longer belong to the WI once they have been given to a church, these are not included in the WI database. The mini sample kneeler from Northamptonshire Federation loan collection is a welcome inclusion.

In the 1980s the 'Community Quilts' project led to co-operative quilt making on a large scale. This was a part of the 'Women in the Community' initiative which culminated in a huge 'Life and Leisure' exhibition at Olympia in 1984. WIs were encouraged to work as a group, include non members, and make a quilt to be exhibited and sold at Olympia. 35% of the money raised from the sale of a quilt was given back to the makers to be used for a WI activity, a special meeting, or some local community project. 550 quilts were made and were a most attractive feature of the exhibition.

Kneeler sample. Northamptonshire FWI
Part of the Federation loan collection, used to demonstrate the different stitches and construction method.
16 canvas with tapisserie wool and stranded cotton threads

1984. Community Quilts on show at Denman College

Stumpwork picture. 1999. Stony Stratford WI. Buckinghamshire
This wall hanging was designed and made by Gill Williams and other Institute members for the Buckinghamshire Federation's 'Life in Today's Community' exhibition. It went on to the NFWI's 'Craft Spectacular' exhibition for the Millennium at Tatton Park in 2000.
Stumpwork figures and buildings in mixed materials

Another common project undertaken by WIs which often encompasses the whole community is the production of a village wall hanging for the village hall or church.

These have been made to celebrate many different events such as Jubilees and new buildings. Initiatives from the NFWI and other organisations have resulted in village 'tapestries'. A great many were made to celebrate the Millennium and are recorded with the NNA. The majority of these projects were undertaken in association with other village groups.

Wall panels. 1946. Painswick WI. Gloucestershire
The panels, depicting the Four Seasons, were designed by Miss Joan West and made by 13 members of the Institute. The five panels took three years to make, and the background to the panels was made entirely out of blackout materials. This panel is 'Spring'. The panels are housed in the Town Hall.
Appliqué and embroidery using mixed fabrics

Wall Hanging. 'Local Life Past and Present' 1984.
Audlem & Buerton WIs. Cheshire
This wall hanging was made for the NFWI 'Life and Leisure' exhibition at Olympia, London in 1984. Predominantly made by Ann Pearce, Yvonne Keen and Jackie Woolsey, many other people helped the project to fruition. As well as Audlem and Buerton, the village of Hankelow is included. Although it does not have a WI, Hankelow is the third village in the parish of St. James the Great, the church where the hanging is housed.
Mixed fabric appliqué mounted on linen

Clothing

WIs have frequently helped other organisations in the village. In 1925, Newbridge on Wye WI, Gwent, reported that it had helped to form a Guide company and made uniforms for the girls, and in other WIs members provided clothes for children in local cottage hospitals. In 1927 WI members began to help some of those most affected by the depression. There were many examples of individual WIs giving help, such as Stoke Edith WI in Herefordshire, which made clothes for distressed miners in South Wales.

The Second World War once more brought the need for WI members to 'make do and mend'. A war time handicraft policy was agreed and WIs were told that they could set up mending parties for evacuee children's clothes, and make garments for the troops, but the materials were not to be bought out of WI funds, the money was to be raised by special effort. One WI member was reported saying that the worst job she had to do was "to mend evacuee boys' trousers." Members knitted 'comforts' for the troops including gloves, socks, balaclavas, knee covers, scarves and jumpers. One unusual area of work done for the Board of Trade was making fur coats from rabbit skins to be sent to Russia. NFWI agreed to support Mrs Churchill's 'Aid to Russia' fur scheme, although this was subsequently seen as more about gaining sympathy for the Russians as allies than actually providing clothing. WI members made coats, waistcoats, hoods and caps lined with rabbit fur for Russian women. Members not only made the clothes but also reared the rabbits and cured the pelts. During two and half years of work 2,071 fur lined garments were sent to Russia via the Red Cross. Mrs Churchill came to the WIs' Consultative Council in 1943 and admired examples of the work. Some garments were also on display at an exhibition organised by the Society for Cultural Relations with USSR.

1923. Paper Pattern

1925. Dressmaking Class

Making fur coats for the Russians

Once the war was over, members knitted and made garments and blankets for refugees and European families in need. There was a similar overwhelming response to an appeal to WI members in 1991. Through a WI member's contact with someone working with children in India, small knitted jumpers were requested. Known as 'Jhuggi Jumpers', they were knitted to a simple pattern in bright and cheerful colours. 25,000 jumpers were knitted, far outreaching the 500 expected. Since 2004 Hampshire WI members have been making basic T shaped jumpers for children in Zimbabwe. They are distributed to orphanages via the Zimbabwe Federation of Women's Institutes and by 2007 more than 4000 had been sent in all colours and sizes.

But the WI doesn't only knit clothes for people, as this report from Bowness WI member Mrs Rosemary Holmes demonstrates:

"The appeal for 'Seabird Sweaters' raised an immediate laugh from our Bowness members. However, patterns were distributed and within two months I had nearly forty multi-coloured ribbed woollen tubes to send to Jim Ward's bird sanctuary at Scarborough."

1940s. Knitting for European relief

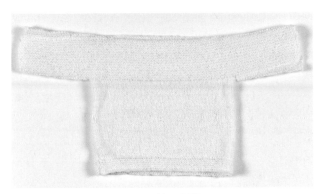

Child's Jumper. 2007. Hampshire FWI
Made by Sue Attrill.

Knitting comforts for the troops
A few rows could be done at any available opportunity.

Seabird Sweaters. Bowness WI. Cumbria Westmorland
This sample is reduced in size, the actual sweaters are for considerably bigger birds!
Ribbed knitting in wool

Jersey and Guernsey Federations endeavour to preserve the tradition of sun bonnet making. This craft used to be a lot more widespread as the picture of the sun bonnet stall at the Royal show in 1927 demonstrates, but the Channel Islanders are keeping their skills alive and patterns are still produced. Dressmakers' paper patterns started to be offered in 'Home and Country' in 1922 and continued until the 1980s. They were mainly for women and children and included garments for sports, household activities, negligees and evening gowns. The nightdress and cap from Lincolnshire North Federation were made in 1922 using a pattern designed and cut by Mrs Faulds. At that time it was very common for dressmakers to cut their own patterns so the introduction of the ready drafted paper pattern made life easier, but also brought more complicated designs within the realm of the home dressmaker. Dressmaking classes used to be very popular and the participants were proud of their efforts as can be seen in the picture of Roffey WI in 1926.

Sun Bonnet. Jersey FWI
Made by Daphne Macready
of Greve dAzette WI.
Cotton gingham

1927. Royal Show. Sun Bonnet stall

Nightdress and Cap. 1922.
Lincolnshire North FWI
Made by Mrs Faulds of
Keddington & Louth Park
WI for the Lincolnshire
Show in 1922 where it was
awarded a Gold Star.
Silk with embroidered
decoration

1922. Paper pattern

1926. Roffey WI. West Sussex
Parade of summer dresses made by members where the materials
cost less than 7s. 6d.

1958. Paper pattern

Making clothes for babies and children had been a necessity for most mothers, and WI loan collections have kept examples of garments and techniques suitable for their decoration.

Cheddar WI, Somerset, took away the trouble and expense of making a Christening set for members' babies by making an Institute set which was rented out for a small fee. It was originally made for an exhibition in Taunton in September 1951 where it won 5 Gold stars and 2 Silver. The set in total is comprised of a robe, petticoat, jacket, bootees, bib, bonnet, coat-hanger and shawl. It is now too delicate to be used.

Raised income levels and the huge import of cheap clothes from overseas has meant a big decline in interest in home dressmaking in recent years. However, creative stitching classes including embroidery and other decorative techniques are still very popular, with course numbers growing every year. Doll making is also growing in popularity once again. When the Clayton-le-Woods WI doll was made, scaled down copies of authentic paper patterns from 'Mabs Fashions', August 1925, were used to make the coat and the underclothes. The doll was made for the Royal Lancashire Show in 1995 and won the Betty Sanderson Memorial Trophy. The doll is 1/5th scale and is used for demonstrations of doll making by its maker, Mrs Mary Margaret Evans.

Baby's Bonnet. c.1960. Cambridgeshire FWI
Made by Mrs Dorothea Jude. Mrs Jude was a tutor and demonstrator for the NFWI, working at Caxton Hall and at WI classes.
Fine linen embroidered using linen lace thread. Hand made tassels and cord

Baby's Dress. 1981. Isle of Wight FWI
Made for the Isle of Wight Federation Diamond Jubilee Exhibition and kept as a craft sample.
Fine cotton lawn

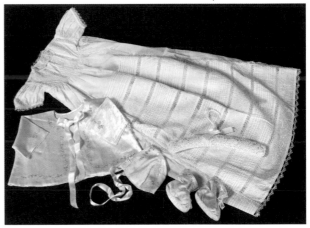

Christening Set. 1951. Cheddar WI. Somerset
The complete set of clothes was made for an exhibition in Taunton in September 1951. It won 5 Gold stars and 2 Silver stars. After that it was hired out for christenings at 10/- a time. A true group effort, nine ladies contributed to the making. The coat-hanger was made from hand made lace in 1989 to display the gown.
Jacket, bonnet & bootees in lined satin. Gown, petticoat & bib in cotton lawn with embroidery, pintucking, and tatted edgings

Doll in 1920's Costume. 1995. Clayton-le-Woods WI. Lancashire
This 1/5th scale model doll was made by Mrs Mary Margaret Evans as a competition entry at the Royal Lancashire Show. The doll was awarded Best in Show. The clothes are scaled down from original contemporary patterns in 'Mabs Fashions'.
Doll made from cotton stuffed with polyester. Clothes made from wool and silk fabrics

Costume

WI members' skills in dressmaking and millinery have not been confined to everyday garments. Choirs, pageants, plays and fancy dress events have all inspired designers and seamstresses.

In 1921, Dunham Massey WI, Cheshire, held a fancy dress ball. The prize for the most original dress was given to the costume illustrating Dunham Massey WI itself; rabbit skins were arranged at the sides and the hat was an old felt hat covered with a little model of the WI hut they intended to buy, with a green lawn around it and a basket work edge.

Throughout the 1920s and 1930s WI choirs were forming; they entertained their fellow WI members and others in the village and took part in local music festivals. Some choirs chose to make a uniform dress. A report on Angel WI choir noted:

"they have an excellent Ladies Choir, and are generally busy in giving concerts for various charities".

Some WIs had folk dance groups and made appropriate costumes for them to wear. These groups are still popular; Gwynedd Caernarfon have a Welsh Folk Dance Group and in East Sussex there is an Elizabethan Dance Group.

'Home and Country' in the interwar years reported that WIs were enjoying fancy dress competitions and entering floats in village carnivals, all showing considerable ingenuity and skill. On the other hand, some of the costumes have been very simple. The set of chefs' hats made for the 1980 carnival float for Sedgeberrow WI, Gloucestershire, were a very basic design but have been used on several occasions since then.

Fancy Dress Costume. 1921. Dunham Massey WI. Cheshire
"Join now and help our Hut Fund".

Choir Costumes. 1921. Angel WI. Pembrokeshire

Smock Costumes for Folk Dancing. 1924. Appledore WI. Kent

Chefs' Hats 1980. Sedgeberrow WI. Gloucestershire
The 'Jammy Dodgers' making jam on the Sedgeberrow WI Carnival Float.
Cotton, machine stitched

Folk Dancing Costumes. 1984. Gwynedd Caernarfon FWI
Made for the Royal Welsh Show 1984 from patterns designed by Mrs Maud Williams, inspired after research done for the Heritage project in 1981. The costumes are used for special events and promotions.
Cotton fabrics

Lancashire Federation float in the Preston Guild procession 1922

In 1980, Welsh Federations made eleven costumes for a Welsh Heritage project. They were all featured in a booklet produced by the Federations of Wales called 'The Welsh Costume'. The costumes were displayed at the Royal Welsh Show and at the National Eisteddfod in 1981. In 2006 only three Federations recorded still having their costumes. The green costume on the left is from Powys Montgomery Federation, and the cocklewoman's costume on the right, made by Mrs Phyllis Rees, is from Glamorgan Federation. The copy of Lady Bevan's 18th century dress, second from left, was made in 1982 by members of Sir Gar Carmarthenshire Federation.

The first record of a WI putting on a play is reported in 'The Landswoman' in November 1918:

"September Meeting of Anstye WI, Sussex, performance of the Mummery by Miss Horn's Company of Mummers who played with great ability Mr Buckett's version of the Tipteerer's play. The dresses which had been made by Miss Horn were correct in every detail."

Miss Horn was the Secretary of the WI and the local school teacher; the drama company were all WI members.

Some dramatic undertakings became more ambitious. In August 1920, in the gardens at Selwood Lodge, Stanwell, Middlesex, the WI put on 'A Midsummer Night's Dream'. Fifty six performers including school children took part and dresses were designed and made by the President and WI members.

The Handicraft Notes in 'Home and Country' thought plays were an ideal opportunity for the whole WI to be involved:

"Making costumes for plays: …while actors are busy studying their parts delightful occupation can be found for every member of the institute who is willing to help. Designing, cutting out and putting together dresses, caps, capes, and headdresses will keep the more skilled dressmakers and milliners busy. The manufacture of trimmings, belts, fringes, jewellery etc. from odds and ends of household waste… will attract younger members…."

Continuing through the 1920s and 1930s many WIs and Federations organised huge outdoor pageants involving the whole community. For the New Forest Pageant at Brockenhurst, Hampshire, the WI members helped to make four hundred and sixty seven costumes and they were offered for sale afterwards. As most of the plays and pageants were depicting historical events, 'Home and Country' carried articles giving advice on what the costumes should look like and how they might be made from simple materials.

Mummers Play. 1918. Anstye WI. Sussex

Drama Banner. Gwent FWI
Made for the old Monmouthshire Federation and depicting a Monmouthshire Trow, this banner was awarded within the Federation for events put on by WIs.
Blue linen. Appliqué

There are several reports of WIs playing 'Living Whist' where people took the part of playing cards. Instructions were given in 'Home and Country' on how to make the outfits. Illustrated is an example from Herefordshire in 1929.

1924. West Kent Federation pageant

In the 1970s East Bridgford WI in Nottinghamshire rediscovered some costumes that had been made many years before and played 'Living Whist' again at a local fete.

Large dramatic events were curtailed during the Second World War but in the 1950s interest was renewed. In 1955 'Home and Country' published articles on *Dressing the Play*; there were drama costume courses at Denman College; and a WI publication, 'Costume, Colour and Cut' by Jeanetta Cochrane, was on sale at a price of 1s 6d. This was in preparation for the National Drama Festival in 1957 for which Robert Gittins had been commissioned by NFWI to write a cycle of plays called 'Out of this Wood', which required historical costumes. In 1969 the composer Malcolm Williamson and librettist Ursula Vaughan Williams created 'The Brilliant and the Dark', an operatic sequence about women's history. 'The Brilliant and the Dark' combined music, drama, dance and handicrafts, and represented the Women's Institutes' first public performance that incorporated so many skills for a National Festival. There were four performances at the Royal Albert Hall when the English Chamber Orchestra, conducted by Marcus Dodds, accompanied 1,300 WI singers. There were one hundred and fifty actors and singers from Hertfordshire and East Sussex Federations. The six hundred costumes were made by WI members to designs by Peter Rice, with fabric donated by Courtaulds.

1929. Living Whist Tabards from Herefordshire

Living Whist Tabards. East Bridgford WI. Nottinghamshire
Hand painted on cotton fabric

The dramatic tradition continues to this day with some very active WIs still doing plays and pantomimes, and Denman College has several drama related courses through the year. Very few WIs recorded having a drama wardrobe in 2006 but some WIs do still keep their own costumes. Eglwysfach WI has a selection of pantomime costumes. These are very simply made but well used.

With the enormous growth of other community clubs and societies in the present day, large organised events in villages and towns tend not to be exclusively run by the WI. However, the local WI is still at the heart of the majority of rural community projects, working with leisure groups, churches, schools and councils.

1969 'The Brilliant and the Dark' performance at the Albert Hall

Pantomime Costumes. 1984/7. Eglwysfach WI. Ceredigion
These costumes were designed and made by Mrs Sheila Latham from recycled clothes and scraps. They are a contemporary example of a WI 'costume cupboard'.
Mixed fabrics and techniques

...and Country

Country Life

Although WIs are now to be found in town and country, the heart of the WI movement in the past lay distinctly in rural communities. WIs were founded to help rural women help themselves, and the emphasis of their work has been in the countryside. It is unsurprising, therefore, that the activities and flavour of rural life can be seen on many of their textiles. Some textiles show a recollection, conscious or unconscious, of the WI's roots as an agricultural institution. Some illustrate the fruits of local agricultural labour, especially if the crop in question is a regional variety or is a well-recognised local livestock breed.

Book Cover. 2000. Upton Bishop WI. Herefordshire
Designed and made by Anne Weedon for the Institute's Millennium year book. It featured in 'Cross Stitch' magazine in February 2001.
Cotton cross stitch on Aida fabric

Banner. c.1925. Longhope. Gloucestershire
This banner was made by Mrs Olive Bowkett and features the 'Blaisdon' plum which was an important product for jam making in the village.
Heavy linen with cotton appliqué, hand embroidery using cotton and silk

Banner. 1937. Leeds WI. West Kent
Hand Embroidery using cotton perle, with cotton appliqué and base fabric

The beehive, which takes pride of place at the centre of the Aperfield WI banner, is depicted alongside a range of mainly textile-based activities, although beekeeping might have been a local pursuit among members in north-west Kent. The name Aperfield itself probably derives from Apple Fields. The Colwall banner features the local 'Colwall' apple variety.

The annual agricultural show marks an important occasion in the life of many rural communities, and the Cheshire Table Screen provided a perfect opportunity to illustrate a range of activities. Commercial enterprises, such as the showing and selling of livestock, take their place alongside shows and competitions involving local produce and handicrafts, both in and out of the marquee. WIs have been taking part in agricultural shows since the WI was started and these occasions are one of the highlights of the rural year.

1922 WI stall at the Royal Bath Show

Table Screen. 1987. Cheshire FWI
The screen was made for the Cheshire Show in 1987 and depicts activities at the show.
Mixed techniques on cotton, mounted on board

Banner. Aperfield WI. West Kent
Sewing symbols and a Traditional Beehive.
Silk Embroidered linen with brocade borders

Banner. 1932. Colwall WI. Herefordshire
Designed and made by Miss Nancy Ballard, the banner won 2nd prize at a Federation competition. It was regularly used at the Giant Picnics held in the County. It shows the Malvern Hills and the Colwall apple.
Felt appliqué on linen fabric with couched wool braids

Events such as these are now recorded on video and in photographs, but their appearance on textiles, which necessarily take a long time to make, is an indication of their perceived importance to the makers of these textile items. However, textile records have a dual purpose as they can be used and serve as constant physical reminders of local heritage while at the same time being robust enough to last, thus taking these records forward to future generations.

Banner. 1924. Steeple Aston WI. Oxfordshire
Designed and made by Miss Dorothea M. Wood who used a live cockerel on the kitchen table as a model for her drawing. St. Peter's cock is the subject of the banner, St. Peter being the patron saint, with St. Paul, of the parish church. The scroll from the beak of the cock was to have 'It is the time to seek the Lord' embroidered on it, but this was never stitched.
Silk embroidery on cotton fabric

Book Cover. Hadlow Green WI. Cheshire
Flowers and Birds of the Wirral Country Park.
Made by members of the Institute.
Embroidered with stranded cottons on linen

Table Cover. 1987. Willesborough WI. East Kent
The cloth depicts local landmarks and was made for the 60th anniversary of the Institute. It was designed by Mrs May Wood and made by 7 members.
Appliqué and embroidery on linen cloth. Windmill sails in cotton crochet

Maps and Histories

Helping to record local events and places is an integral part of the role WIs play in their localities. In photographic scrapbooks and in their record books WIs have noted down what have become detailed histories of people and places, reinforcing the sense of place and belonging that is often associated with WI activities. This sense of place and marking the boundaries is often reflected in WI textiles, sometimes explicitly, such as in representations of village and county maps, sometimes more subtly, in the depiction of aspects of local identity which hint at story or folklore.

Cuckoo. 1995. Eglwyswrw & District. Pembrokeshire
The legend of the cuckoo of Nevern tells how the bird used to appear on the same day in April every year. One year, after the villagers' long wait, the bird arrived very late in the day, then fell dead. This bird was a group entry in a County Competition, and went on to the Royal Welsh Show, winning on both occasions. It was designed by Mrs Cecily Jellyman and made by Mrs Tricia Fox.
Embroidered in satin stitch, the beak is the end of a quill, the claws being wool covered wire

Banner. 1997. Stanton St. John WI. Oxfordshire
Made for the 75th anniversary of the Institute, the banner was designed by Rosemary Money and stitched by her with Ann Nutt and Joyce Roden. It depicts a bluebell wood and the church, plus the building where the first meeting of this Institute was held in 1922.
Hand made felt, painted and embroidered

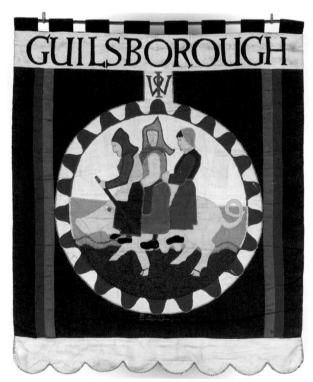

Banner. 1938. Guilsborough WI. Northamptonshire
This banner, made by members of Guilsborough WI, was exhibited at the NFWI Exhibition at the New Horticultural Hall, Westminster, in 1938. It depicts a local legend about 3 witches. In fact, 2 women from Guilsborough were hung as witches at Abingdon in July 1612.
Linen with hand appliquéd images

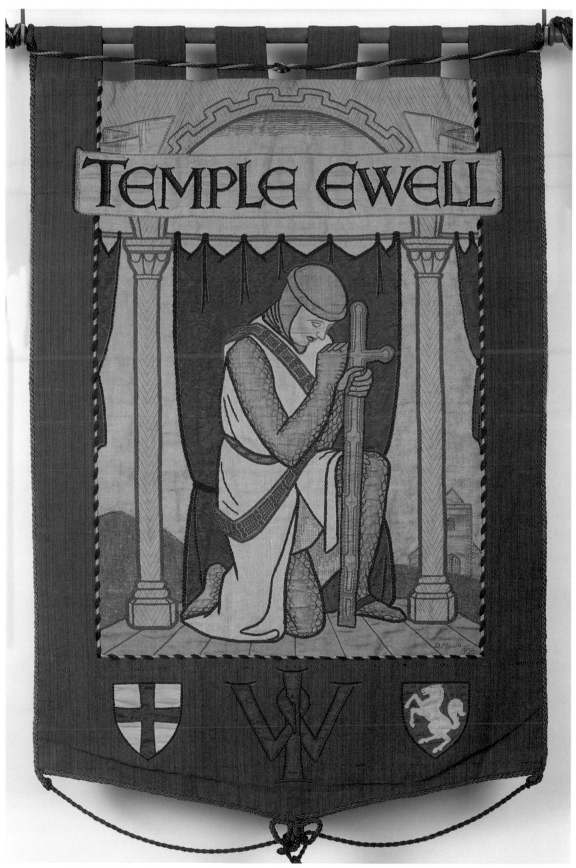

1938. Temple Ewell WI. East Kent
The banner symbolises the close association with the Order of the Knights Templar with the ancient village of
Temple Ewell. The Order built the church in Temple Ewell and its Norman arch is depicted on the banner.
Designed and made by D. Mowll.
Appliqué and embroidery on linen

At first sight, the Trumpington WI banner does not appear to have much of a story to tell. However, the juxtaposition of the WI emblem and local insignia, in this case the coat of arms of the 13th century Crusader from whom the village takes its name, is a familiar theme in WI textiles which show an awareness of their locality and its history. Similarly, Northaw WI's banner depicts King James I who took the land around the village as part of his hunting grounds. The banner also shows Northaw WI's 1917 founding date – the oldest WI in Hertfordshire.

Banner. 1956. Lydd. East Kent
The Lydd banner depicts the town seal with pictures of the town's history and features of the area including Romney marsh sheep and Dungeness lighthouse. Designed by Miss Done and Miss A. Hayward, and worked by members of the Institute.
Appliqué on linen

Banner. Trumpington WI. Cambridge
Possibly made in the 1930s, the first record of the banner is at the Institute's 30th anniversary party in 1950.
Heavy canvas work with additional hand embroidery

Banner. c.1933. Northaw WI. Hertfordshire
Designed by Leslie Church and worked by Ursula Church, President of the Institute from 1930 – 1936.
Silk embroidery on linen

104

Federation and village parish maps lend themselves well to being portrayed in fabric and stitches. The results are hard wearing and their flexibility means easy handling if the map is on a very large scale. This method of recording maps is not new and these examples show that WI maps have been popular for many years.

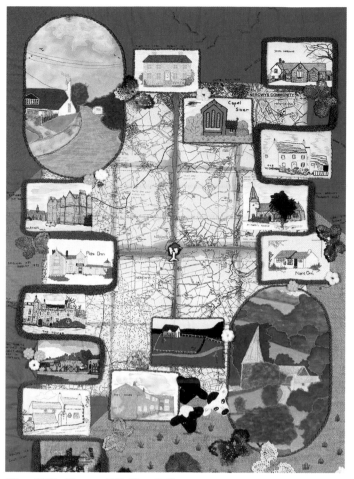

Map. 1999. Nercwys WI. Clwyd Flint
Made by 13 members of the Institute craft group to celebrate the Millennium, the map was entered in a County competition. It was designed by Hazel Holker and depicts local landmarks and fauna.
Cotton based with applied images in a variety of techniques including knitting, canvas work, cross stitch. Map photo-transferred onto calico

Book Cover. 1951. Church Minshull WI. Cheshire
Made by Mrs K. Grimes for a competition, the book gained commendations for its originality. Recently lost, it was found again.
Linen hand embroidered with stranded cottons

Table Cover. 1937. Hellesdon WI. Norfolk
A map of old Hellesdon showing the meeting hall of the WI. 77 signatures of members on the outer bricks.
Cotton embroidery on linen

County Map. Buckinghamshire FWI
Discovered at a car boot sale in the mid 1990s and given to Buckinghamshire Federation. Made sometime between 1949 and 1975.
Cotton embroidery on linen fabric

Some textile 'documents' are more reminiscent of snapshots than cartography, with representations of village scenes and buildings intended to capture the essence of village life, rather than map out its boundaries.

Table Cover (detail). c.1965. Guernsey FWI
Designed by Mrs Sheila Lintell and made by members of the Institutes. The cloth depicts local landmarks and was made for the 60th anniversary of the Federation.
Appliqué and embroidery on linen fabric

Hayes WI banner in the 1950s

Banner. c.1920. Hayes Morning. West Kent
All records prior to 1945 for this Institute were lost so no early details about this banner exist.
Felt appliqué covered in blue net

Banner. 1989. Flaxley WI. Gloucestershire
The banner features Flaxley Abbey, previously a Cistercian monastery, which is a major building in this village. Local Flora and Fauna are shown including the 'Blaisdon Red' plum. Designed and made by Susan Mitchell with Mesdames Armitage, Bowers, Hughes, N. Young and R. Young.
Embroidery cottons on linen fabric

Table Cover. 1949. Salfords WI. Surrey
This cloth was designed by Miss Fraser and made for the 21st Anniversary of the Institute. Based on a 1928 picture of the village, it was stitched by every member. Mrs Lavender, an LCC teacher of Embroidery, oversaw the making of the cloth and she was presented with a leather handbag at the unveiling.
Cotton embroidery on linen

Book Cover. 1958. Marcham WI. Oxfordshire
Made by several members to celebrate the 10th anniversary of the re-forming of the Institute in 1948. The book cover is a copy of the WI's banner. There are 16 dovecotes in Marcham dating from pre 17th century. The book cost 9s 11d to make.
Felt appliqué and embroidery on felt background

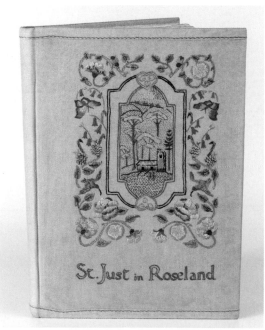

Book Cover. 1951. St. Just in Roseland WI. Cornwall
Designed by Mrs Butland and Mrs Couch. A contemporary scrapbook about St. Just in 1951 which is now a fascinating history. The cover portrays the church. The book was made as an entry to the Cornwall Federation Baker Cup competition and formed part of a display at the Royal Show. It subsequently featured in a BBC TV programme.
Embroidery cottons on linen

Book Cover. 1981. Appleby Magna WI.
Leicestershire and Rutland
In 1981 the Leicestershire Diocese commissioned Federation WIs to make an inventory of churchyard headstones. This is the record of the stones in St. Michael and All Angels Church, Appleby Magna. The book cover was made by Mrs Marion Hunt.
Heavy linen fabric with cross stitch in stranded cotton

Citizenship

Lady Denman felt that ordinary countrywomen had an important part to play in the development of rural life. She wanted to open the WI members' eyes to a wider vision and to work for things that would not only improve their lives and those of their families, but would also help the wider community. The Government too, was very supportive of initiatives that would bring economic growth and social improvement to rural areas and it supported the WIs financially. Once the First World War was over and providing food was no longer the main priority, the Women's Institute movement pursued its two central aims of improving the conditions of rural life and providing for the further education of countrywomen.

Helping newly enfranchised women to understand how they could take their part in public life and influence the decision makers was important in the early years. The increasing numbers of WIs meant that over the years the movement has been strong enough to make a difference on social issues and to give a countrywide relevance to all its policies. Both the organisational growth and the campaigning aspect of their work can be seen reflected in WI textiles. Individual WIs such as Melbury Osmund WI, have produced inspiring banners, and the NFWI hierarchy is represented in group and Federation banners.

Banner. c.1921.
Melbury Osmond WI. Dorset
Institute banner, thought to have been made near the founding date of the Institute in 1921.
Appliqué on linen

Banner. 1965. Datchet WI. Berkshire
Group banner for the Swan Group of WIs. Made by Phil Taylor, Queenie Sams and Brenda Reader.
Canvas work

Banner. 1974. Sir Gar Carmarthenshire
Federation banner made by Vida Wood.
Appliqué and embroidery on grosgrain fabric

WI members were encouraged to take part in public life and to have representatives on Parish and District Councils. From its first 'public affairs' resolution on State Aided Housing which was adopted in 1918, the WI was committed to its work of entering into a dialogue with Government to bring about improvements. This has remained a central feature of WI work, resulting in a long list of campaigns. During the 1920s alone, campaigns for women jurors, film censorship, humane animal slaughter, reducing oil pollution and anti-litter were all supported. New mandates have been adopted every year and the WIs' campaigning zeal is renowned. National campaigns have inspired competition themes such as 'a picture depicting an endangered species', and 'Save our Heritage'. One national competition based on environmental issues was 'This Green and Pleasant Land ?' The question mark reflected the concern that WI members felt about the future of the countryside. WIs were invited to depict this idea and there were competitions at Federation level. Some of the regional winners were displayed in the Pillar Hall at Olympia, as part of the Ideal Home Exhibition in 1972.

Picture. 1970. Shincliffe WI. Durham
One of a set of four, these pictures were designed and made by Miss L.C. Anderson for the County round of the 'This Green and Pleasant Land?' competition, where they were the regional winner. The pictures show Dereliction, Desolation, Reclamation and Transformation. They were accepted by Beamish Museum but never displayed and they now hang in the WI hall in Shincliffe.
Linen base with painting, raw edge appliqué, net overlay and worked with a variety of canvas stitches in wool

Picture. 1975.
Hadlow Green WI. Cheshire
Heritage Year exhibit made by Mrs M. Annetts.
Felt appliqué on cotton

Picture. Kennington WI. East Kent
Made by members of the Institute's handicraft group for a competition entry depicting endangered species. Displayed at Arundel Wildfowl Trust in 1983.
Wool with felt appliqué and hand embroidery

Wall Plaques. 1984. Gwynedd Caernarfon FWI
Part of the 'Women in the Community' set of wall plaques made for the Royal Welsh Agricultural Show, showing aspects of Health, Education and Community.
WI members campaigning. Concern over land fill sites. Campaign to support Dairy Farmers and preserve doorstop milk deliveries.
A variety of canvas work stitches and techniques in wool

During the depression of the 1930s, many ordinary members of WIs would, of course, themselves have been affected by the economic situation. However, the officers and members of the National Executive Committee were predominantly from the aristocracy and monied classes and they felt that WIs should do whatever they could to help areas of unemployment. It was resolved at the AGM in 1934: "That since it is the policy of the NFWI to promote the teaching of handicrafts for home-making and as a leisure time occupation, and since the present high standard of craft work in the WIs would not have been attained but for the generous grants of money received for this purpose from HM Government, this meeting endorses the action of the Executive Committee in agreeing as a method of national service to administer for a limited period a special grant to assist in the teaching of such crafts in Occupational Centres for the unemployed"

At these centres WI members who had qualified through the WI tutoring schemes taught craft skills such as making thrift rugs to unemployed people. It was stressed that this project was to provide occupation for the unemployed to make things for their own use and not for sale. Local enterprise was not being encouraged.

1930s. Demonstrating making thrift rugs to unemployed workers
The rugs were often made from woollen scraps dyed with vegetable dyes.

This history of WI campaigns is often celebrated at Federation events. The Dunston, Hyde Lea and Coppenhall WI banner was made from scrap fabrics for a Staffordshire parade in 1989 and depicts the adoption in 1926 of the Norfolk Federation's resolution to support the National Savings scheme by establishing savings groups.

Banner. 1989. Dunston with Hyde Lea and Coppenhall WI. Staffordshire
Designed by Sylvia Wood and Marjory Blundy for the SFWI 70th anniversary garden party.
Mixed appliqué on polyester cotton fabric machine stitched

Other events have also been recorded in textile pictures. In 1988 the WI's first appearance at the Chelsea Flower Show brought great success. 'The Countrywoman's Garden', designed by a Cheshire member and built by Bridgemere Garden World, won not only a Gold Medal but also the Wilkinson's Sword of Honour. A canvas work pattern was produced of the garden for members.

Picture. 1988. Bancffosfelen WI. Sir Gar Carmarthenshire
Picture of the NFWI's winning Chelsea garden.
Made by Diane Hardy, President of Bancffosfelen WI, and given to the Institute in her memory, by her mother.
Wool canvas work

The WIs were extremely active during both World Wars helping with the war effort. On the home front members grew and sold food, made clothes, shoes and furniture; they mended them and made them last. Women all over the country were also engaged in doing the jobs the men could no longer do such as delivering the post and working on public transport, while others made munitions, and stitched camouflage nets.

The making of these nets is one of the occupations depicted on 'Women's Work in Wartime'. This is a large canvas work wall hanging housed at the Imperial War Museum. In 1946 the WI decided to record the work done by women during the war and started work on this embroidery. The finished hanging was displayed at the Victoria and Albert Museum where it took pride of place at the WI exhibition of handicrafts in March 1952. Designed by Sybil Blunt, the hanging measures 15ft 3in by 9ft. Work started at three embroidery schools held in Winchester. At these schools the canvas stitches were taught to a representative from each county, who then taught other members, and eventually about four hundred selected embroiderers contributed. The actual work on the canvas hanging itself started in 1947 and it took about four years to complete. Stitched across the foot of the hanging is a quotation from Shakespeare's Henry VIII: "The Madams too not used to Toil did almost Sweat to bear the Pride upon them."

After the close of the exhibition at the V&A the wall hanging then travelled to eighteen counties, to Edinburgh for a meeting of the Scottish Rural Institutes, and to the Countrywomen of Australia. Finally it was deposited at the Imperial War Museum in 1955. It was displayed for a while but then in the early 1970s it was taken to the Imperial War Museum store at Duxford near Cambridge. It was put on display again in the early 1990s as well as at an exhibition of 'Women At War' in the early 2000s, before being returned to Duxford for storage.

One of the Winchester sewing schools making 'Women's Work in Wartime'

Detail: Women in Industry

Detail: Making Camouflage Nets

'Women's Work in Wartime'
Made by WI members and now at the Imperial War Museum.
Wool on canvas

Another very large embroidered picture with which WIs were involved was designed by Constance Howard for the Festival of Britain in 1951. Commissioned by the organisers for the Countryside Pavilion, 'The Country Wife' depicts the crafts and activities of the WI at that time. The mural was designed and made by Constance with Goldsmiths' College students; the various craft pieces being made by experts from the WI. The whole work was made at a scale of five eighths actual size and is mainly stumpwork and appliqué. The mural measures 5 metres by 4.5 metres. It was too large to be completely assembled in the studio and had to be finished at the Festival site. During the Festival many of the smaller items such as the embroidered fish in the frying pan were stolen and had to be replaced several times. At the end of the exhibition the embroidery was given to the NFWI. The mural was transported in one piece packed in a large crate, on the back of a very large lorry. On arrival at Denman College, where it was to be housed, neither the lorry nor the crate would go through the front gate and a crane had to be employed to lift the crate over the wall. Fortunately, the journey was successfully accomplished and the mural has been at Denman ever since.

1951. 'The Country Wife'

Over the years WIs have produced special books such as visitor books, presentation books, scrap books and record books reflecting the activities of the Institute and providing an invaluable source of contemporary observation and data. Many of these books have had textile worked covers. Local newspapers have regularly reported WI events, and many WIs kept these cuttings; some stuck them in the WI Record book and others kept them in a scrap book and added photographs and other memorabilia. These books are now of considerable archival value. As well as recording the history of the WI, scrapbooks have also recorded the history of the village. From time to time the NFWI has stimulated this interest by holding a book competition. The first of these was launched by National Vice Chairman Grace Hadow in October 1921. She asked WIs to compile Institute books to record local history, customs and folk lore and offered a prize. By March 1922 over 50 books were entered and Dr Marett, Reader in Anthropology at Oxford University, judged them. He commented "if we can keep these books carefully we shall be doing something of real value to historians."

The next national competition for WI Scrapbooks was in the Golden Jubilee year of 1965. The idea was to record village life for a year. 2,600 WIs compiled books and each Federation selected 3 to be sent to London for judging, where they were displayed at the 'The Countrywoman Today' exhibition held at the Ceylon Tea Centre. Many of these scrapbooks had beautifully embroidered covers.

1965. Judging the scrapbooks

Book Cover. 1965. Melbury Osmond WI. Dorset
Made for the NFWI Jubilee scrapbook project, the bookcover won a prize in the Dorset County competition.
Cotton patchwork with embroidered details

Book Cover. 1965. Leigh WI. Surrey
Made for the NFWI Golden Jubilee scrapbook project by Mrs Kaye and Mrs Harries.
Cross stitch on linen

Royalty

The WI has always supported, and been supported by, the female members of the Monarchy. Queen Mary was the first Royal WI member and she became the President of Sandringham WI, Norfolk. Traditionally, this post is now always held by the first lady of the land. All members of the Royal family who join the WI are fully paid up members.

WI textiles have commemorated Royal events in many different techniques. The crochet picture of the Queen was made for the 'Tomorrow's Heirlooms' exhibition in 1972 and is kept in the East Kent Federation office.

Unusually, commemorative rugs have been made by members of Aston Ingham WI, Herefordshire for the coronation of George VI in 1937 and by Shottisham WI, Suffolk East for the coronation of Elizabeth II in 1953. Both of these rugs have been in continuous use by their WIs since they were made.

Picture. 1972. East Kent FWI
Made by Alice Simpson, the crochet picture of the Queen was entered in the 'Tomorrow's Heirlooms' exhibition.
Cotton crochet

Rug. 1937. Aston Ingham WI. Herefordshire
This rug was made by members of the Institute to celebrate the Coronation of King George VI. The rug is placed in front of the President's table at each meeting. The Institute are currently researching the initials around the edge of the rug.
Wool on rug canvas

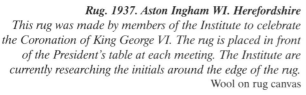

Rag Rug. c.1953.
Shottisham WI. East Suffolk
Designed and worked by Mrs Mabel Emmens to celebrate the Coronation. For many years the rug was kept in front of the coal fire at the Trust Hall until being rescued, washed, and displayed as a wall hanging.
Recycled fabrics on Hessian

Commemorative banners are widespread, but most popular are table covers marking special Royal events including the Coronation, Silver and Golden Jubilees and Royal weddings.

Table Cover. 1953. Mattingley WI. Hampshire
Designed by Mrs Murphy and worked by her with other members of the Institute to celebrate the Coronation.
Cotton embroidery on linen fabric

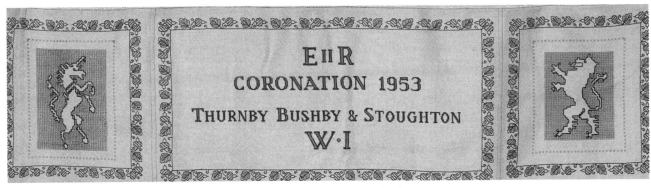

EIIR
CORONATION 1953
THURNBY BUSHBY & STOUGHTON
W·I

Table Cover. 1953. Thurnby Bushby & Stoughton WI. Leicestershire and Rutland
The work on this cloth began in September 1953 to celebrate the Coronation and it was first used at the 21st birthday party of the Institute in 1956. Designed by Margaret Smith, it depicts the Queen's Beasts being the Lion of England, the Unicorn of Scotland, the Black Bull of Clarence, the White Horse of Hanover and the Falcon of the Plantagenets.
Cream silk hand woven by Dreda Smith, Assisi Embroidery by Institute members

Banner. 1953.
Horndean WI.
Hampshire
Made by the Horndean WI Craft Group to a design by Mrs K.F. Webb to commemorate the Coronation, and incorporating local landmarks.
Linen fabric with satin border worked in embroidery silks and cottons

Banner. 1953. Gaunts & Holt WI. Dorset
Designed by Mrs Harvey-Murray and worked by Mrs Hough.
Embroidery cottons on heavy linen fabric

Picture. 2002. Sarisbury Green WI. Hampshire
*'Waiting for the Queen', designed by Hilary Gardner
and worked by members of the Institute. This started
off as a simple exercise in making stumpwork faces but
grew into a celebration of the Queen's Golden Jubilee.*
Mixed fabrics with polyester wadding, vilene and old tights

Handkerchief. 1953. Bassingham WI. Lincolnshire South
*Printed souvenir purchased in 1953 and kept by the
Institute among their treasures for over fifty years.*
Cotton

Table Screen. 2005. North Tawton Afternoon WI. Devon
*Other 'Queens' are commemorated too. This tryptych was made as part of the Institute's display at the Okehampton Show where it
won first prize. Designed and made by Gisela Banbury, it depicts the launching of the liner 'QM2'.*
Silks on a cotton background, mounted on hardboard. Appliqué and machine embroidery

A World View

The English and Welsh WIs have never broken the early bond with the Canadian WI movement and from time to time members visit Stoney Creek, birthplace of the WI in Ontario. Tea towels are a popular souvenir gift for the WI 'back home'. Another example of a souvenir kept by Bishopswood WI is a fine silk scarf from the 1956 Olympic Games in Melbourne, Australia.

Olympic Games Scarf. 1956. Bishopswood WI. Herefordshire
This Institute has been corresponding with Murrumbeena A.C.W.W. from 1953 to the present day. When the Olympic Games were held in Melbourne in 1956, Murrumbeena sent this souvenir scarf to Bishopswood.
Dyed silk chiffon

Tea Towel. Wyberton WI. Lincolnshire South
Commercially printed tea towel from Stoney Creek in Canada, the birthplace of the WI movement.
Printed cotton

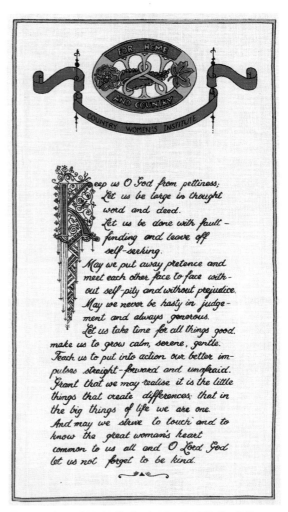

Tea Towel. c. 1988. Rollesby & District WI. Norfolk
A commercially produced souvenir tea towel from Canada.
Printed linen

Women's Institutes now operate in many different countries in the world. English and Welsh WIs maintain links with WIs in other countries, and exchange gifts. In 1955 Alrewas WI in Staffordshire made a quilt of 2,111 pieces and presented it to the Dutch Countrywomen's Association after they had hosted a visit.

Women's organizations have flourished around the world and in 1929 'The Associated Country Women of the World' (ACWW) was formed. ACWW now has a membership of nine million through its 365 Member Societies in over 70 countries. Almost all NFWI Federations are members of the ACWW and representatives travel to conferences and events all over the world.

Table Cover (detail). 1964. Wendover Afternoon WI.
Buckinghamshire
Made by Mrs Nell Gynne in Australia as a gift to
Wendover Afternoon WI at Christmas 1964.
The cloth features Australian flora and fauna.
Hand embroidered cotton embroidery on linen with
crochet edging

Table Cover. c.1960. Hollingbourne WI. West Kent
A gift from Whakatane WI, New Zealand showing
New Zealand birds and flowers.
Cotton embroidery on linen

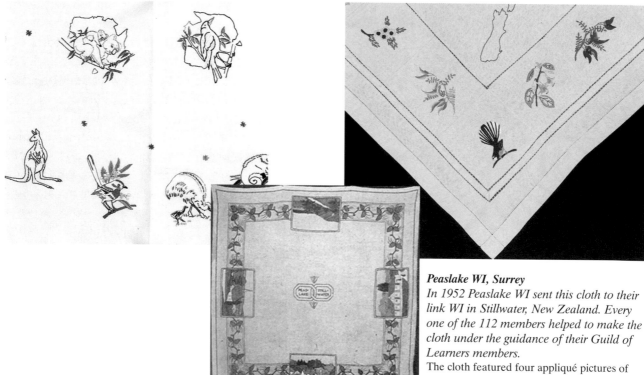

Peaslake WI, Surrey
In 1952 Peaslake WI sent this cloth to their
link WI in Stillwater, New Zealand. Every
one of the 112 members helped to make the
cloth under the guidance of their Guild of
Learners members.
The cloth featured four appliqué pictures of
local scenes on a border of pine cones and
foliage

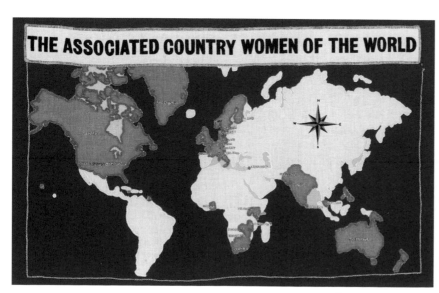

Table Cover. 1961. Rumburgh WI.
Suffolk East
Cloth depicting the scope of the
Association of Country Women of the
World. It was made by cutting out the
land shapes from a pre-printed ACWW
tea towel and appliquéing them onto a
background fabric.
Appliquéd cotton on cotton background
fabric

Conclusion

The previous chapters have looked at the range of textiles owned by the WI. Some are beautifully worked, some are eccentric, and all make a significant contribution to the overall collection. And that is the important thing to remember, it is a 'Collection', even if the artefacts themselves are not necessarily collected together in one place. One of the primary objectives of the National Needlework Archive is to curate and protect textile artefacts and collections such as that belonging to the WI. Typically, these are collections where the artefacts are distributed widely across the country and yet form an integral part of an important unified 'whole'. Needlework has been a central feature of the work of the Women's Institutes since the inception of the movement and this has led to one of the largest and potentially most interesting collections of 20th century textiles in the UK. The NNA and the NFWI agreed that, since no structured or comprehensive catalogue of the collection had ever been made, it was important that this national collection should be recorded. The collection is a valuable textile and social resource, which forms a substantial part of the nation's craft and artistic history. It is also at risk, and one of the aims of the project is to raise awareness with WI members themselves about the value of what they own, while at the same time raising the profile of the work to a wider audience. A fully documented and photographic record of the collection will help to reduce losses and improve storage conditions.

The value of preserving the commonplace as well as the best of textiles which form part of an overall picture of organisational, or social, history has been demonstrated. The Textile Recording Project for the WI is ongoing and as new WIs are opened, and existing Institutes flourish, the new textiles they produce will begin to shape the nature of the 21st century's textile story. As older WIs close, one of the important lessons from this project is the need to be increasingly vigilant that their textiles do not vanish with them. Textile heritage that is lost, and the repertoire of textile skills that are lost with it, cannot be easily reclaimed. Preservation and renewal are more effective than attempts at recollection and reconstruction. It is to be hoped that WIs and Federations that have not yet recorded their textile holdings will be inspired by what they have read in this book, and it will encourage them to complete their return, and so add another stitch to the fabric of the WI's heritage knowledge. New textiles are best recorded when they are new and memories fresh. Searching for ill-recorded information, generations later, can produce unreliable material.

The NNA is always keen to find out about textiles, including banners and table covers, from closed WIs. These may be in homes, local museums, or churches, but it is helpful to know where they are so their whereabouts can be recorded, and this will also help to preserve them. Textiles are lost from existing WIs too. It is a debateable point whether banners and table covers, for instance, are safer in a cupboard in a village hall, or in a member's house. On the face of it, a private house, which is warm, dry, and generally undisturbed, would be seen as safer than a village hall which may be cold and damp, may have vermin, and which is used by dozens of disparate groups over a week, all with possible access to the textiles. Banners and cloths do get stolen and damaged. However, our work has shown that by far the greatest hazard to WI textiles is being taken home to members' houses and, for whatever reason, not being returned. These are not malicious or underhand actions. The items are taken home to genuinely safeguard and care for them. However, it is easy to forget about things; one table cover was at the back of a member's airing cupboard for twelve years and a new one made before it came to light, much to the member's embarrassment! A new President or Secretary doesn't necessarily know what should be transferred to her when she takes office, and it may be many years before an Institute realises that something isn't around anymore. Collective memory often struggles when having to delve back fifteen years or more to the last time anyone remembers seeing an old cloth. Also, members may unfortunately pass away while being in charge of WI items, and families clearing houses very often throw them away because they don't know what they are, or to whom they should be returned. To avoid scenarios such as these, follow the guidelines at the end of this chapter to safeguard textiles in trust.

Storing the textiles is another consideration. Banners are best kept covered and hung up when not in use to prevent creasing and distortion. If this is not possible then rolling is better than folding. Roll the banner over a large roll and not just around its top pole which is too thin, and means the fabric on the banner gets pushed downwards, resulting in unsightly creasing at the bottom of the banner. A cardboard tube, padded out with clean old towels or polyester wadding to a diameter of about 4" will be satisfactory for rolling most banners around. The banner should be rolled with the front face out, again to reduce creasing to the best side. Wrap it in acid free tissue paper, or a piece of clean white cotton sheeting, and *gently* tie two or three pieces of very wide white cotton tape around it to stop it unrolling. Keep it in an acid free box or specially made bag – clearly and firmly labelled on the outside.

Table covers too, are best kept rolled rather than folded, and this also saves on ironing before meetings. Wrap a cardboard or plastic tube in polyester wadding and acid free tissue paper before rolling the table cover around it. If it is unavoidable for cloths to be folded, they should regularly be refolded in different ways to prevent the fabric becoming brittle and splitting, which eventually happens if the folds always come in the same place.

Embroidered book covers, work boxes and other similar items should be padded with acid free tissue or polyester wadding where necessary and kept in boxes to prevent distortion. If the pages of the books are not acid free, slip loose leaves of acid free paper between the pages and the covers. Keep an eye on these leaves of acid free paper; if they start to discolour then the fabric covers are at risk of staining from the book contents. At the very least, replace the acid free paper leaves with new clean ones on a frequent and regular basis.

Heritage items require a long term view. It is often difficult to know, when an item is new, whether it will become important or not. The

work of artists who become famous, iconic items of an age, examples of teaching methods, or one item of many which illustrate a style development; they all play their part and are represented in the WI Textile Collection. In this book we have seen how, over the past century, textile activities have been shaped by the prevailing aspects and attitudes of our culture; post-war austerity, make-do-and-mend, never-had-it-so-good, enlightened self-interest, and the throw-away society with embroidered table covers often being replaced with paper cloths on a roll. We cannot tell what cultural influences will be most pervasive or influential on our textile heritage as the 21st century unfolds. What is abundantly clear from our research is that a lack of design and skill instruction at a basic foundation level is having a devastating effect on the quality of community textiles. This affects the WI too. Taking banners as an example, it is easy to find many from the 1920s and 1930s which have a good, coherent overall design, are beautifully worked, and are hard wearing. These features are much harder to find in new banners. The same is true for table covers, the most rapidly growing sector of WI-owned textiles. In the community as a whole, the need for basic design guidelines and good technique training is apparent. However, WIs are among the few organisations in the UK which are making institutional textiles on a major scale and some of the more modern items are set to become the wonderful 'treasures' of the future. The wide range of skills and areas of expertise exhibited in the collection is amazing, and each area is backed by years of WI dedication to raising standards and preserving traditions.

Recording textiles is the best way to trace related trends and to preserve skills and ideas. The NNA and the NFWI are well on the way to producing a comprehensive database of WI textiles across the country which will be of value both to WIs, and to a wide research population in textiles, social and art history, and women's studies. This recording also acts to protect the artefacts themselves by raising their perceived value in the eyes of their custodians. In the long term, the value of being able to study the NFWI Textile Collection as a unified body of work will be substantial. The opportunity to see some of these beautiful textiles exhibited together in 'Textile Treasures of the WI' is a delight.

Golden Rules for Safeguarding WI textiles:

Always store items in a well defined and recognisable box or custom-made storage bag which is clearly and firmly labelled on the inside and outside with:

- 'This *(insert description of item e.g. banner/ table cover)* is the property of *(insert name of WI)* and should be returned to them or the *(insert name of Federation)* Federation, tel. no. *(insert telephone number.)*'

   Wherever possible, the item itself should also carry a stitched or pencil written label, saying the same thing.

- One member of the Institute committee should be appointed to be responsible for keeping the inventory of textiles up to date for the Institute and the NNA; for knowing where they are, and actually inspecting them on a regular basis. This need take only a few minutes. At each Annual General Meeting a short report of a few sentences on their whereabouts and condition will ensure that no more than twelve months can go by before things are missed.

- Textile items no longer required should be offered to the Federation, Denman College or the dedicated WI Collection at the NNA for safe keeping.

- **NEVER** store textiles in black plastic bin bags. Textiles shouldn't be kept in plastic bags at all, but if it is absolutely necessary to keep an item in a plastic bag for a short period of time, it should be in a clear plastic bag so that the contents can be clearly identified, and well labelled as above.

Record of the making of a 1996 Table Cover by Darfield WI. South Yorkshire
This compilation of notes, fabric and stitch samples, design drawings and lots of photos, was compiled by Mrs A. Mellor to record the design and making of the Darfield 10th anniversary cloth. Full of practical and social information, it is a valuable addition to the NNA's WI archive.

Banner. (detail) 1928. Cannington WI. Somerset

Book Cover. 1982. Edlesborough WI. Buckinghamshire
This book was made by Mrs Julie Blackwell. The cover depicts the rose brass of Edlesborough, made in 1412 for the church, with the Buckinghamshire swan emblem. A member's husband made a carved oak box especially for the book.
Velvet with felt appliqué with white and gold embroidery

Table Cover (detail) c.1958. West Chiltington WI. West Sussex
Each square of the cover was individually made by members of West Chiltington WI.
Evenweave cotton fabric with beige cotton cross stitch embroidery in folkweave patterns

Bibliography

Beck, Thomasina — **The Embroiderer's Story.** Needlework from the Renaissance to the Present Day. 1999 David & Charles.

Christie, Mrs A.H. — **Samplers and Stitches,** A Handbook of the Embroiderer's Art 4th ed. 1948

Goodenough, Simon — **Jam and Jerusalem.** A pictorial history of Britain's greatest women's movement. 1977. NFWI

Gorman, John — **Banner Bright.** 1973. Penguin Books

Howard, Constance — **20th Century Embroidery in Great Britain** 4 volumes B.T. Batsford Ltd.

Jenkins, Inez — **History of the Women's Institute Movement of England and Wales** 1953. Oxford University Press

Kaye, Barbara — **Live and Learn.** The Story of Denman College 1948-1969 NFWI 1970

Pass, Olivia — **Dorset Feather Stitchery.** 2nd ed. 1958. Jarrold & Sons Ltd.

Robertson Scott, J.W — **History of the WI.** 1925. The Village Press

Stamper, Anne — **Rooms off the Corridor.** Education in the WI and 50 years of Denman College. 1948-1998. 1998. NFWI

c.1928. Church Stretton WI. Shropshire
Designed by Mrs Walker, this banner is now used mainly as a table frontal at meetings.
Embroidered in wool on a heavy linen base fabric

Photo Credits

Many of the photographs in this book were taken by Andy Brown Photography (Romsey, Hampshire). A number are also reproduced from photos provided by the NFWI.

The publishers also wish to acknowledge the assistance they received in locating and reproducing a number of other photographs and illustrations, which are included within this book by kind permission of the following individuals, Institutes and Federations. Where no credit is given, it is because it has not proved possible to identify the copyright holder. The publishers will be happy to rectify, in any future printings, any errors and omissions brought to their attention.

Banbury, Gisela	North Tawton WI, p116
Bartley, Judith	Leigh WI, p113
Blow, Thea	The Lee WI, p27
Braiden, Elizabeth M	Edlesborough WI, p63, p122
Burgess, Jean	Lincs Nth FWI p14, p15, p92
Burrows, Christine	Northaw WI, p104
Bush, Richard	Cockpole Green WI, p41
Caesley, R	Melbury Osmond WI, p113
Callender, R M	Willaston WI, p23
Chellaston WI	Chellaston WI, p44
Colehill Evening WI	Colehill Evening WI, p65
Connell, Linda	Fox doll p87, Sutton Green WI p86, Oxford FWI sampler p83, Sashes p30, West Malling WI detail p4l, Wells WI p63, Twyford WI detail p64, Country Wife p112, Mattingley WI detail p115
Corke, Gill	St John's Evening WI, p27
Culshaw, David	Llay WI, p25
Dennison, Beryl	Sanderstead WI, p34
Dodd, Kay	Guernsey FWI, p106
Edwards, Jill	Mickleover WI, p33
Edwards, S	Marcham WI, p107
Evans, E A	Bridport Centre WI, p60
Farmer, C L	Northants FWI, p35
Ferguson, E G	Abbots Bromley WI, p30
Forbes, Hilary	Penn & Tylers Green WI, p34
Gardner, Hilary	Sarisbury Green WI, p116
Gaunts and Holt WI	Gaunts & Holt WI, p115
Gilkes, Susan	Brailes WI, p38
Good, F	Stony Stratford WI, p88
Grattan-Guiness, Enid	Bengeo WI, p41
Harris, B	Broome WI, p44
Harrop, R F	Lockswood WI, p45
Head, Katrina	Thornton WI, p26
Hewitt, Pamela	Sedgeberrow WI, p94
Hodges, Brian	Dunston with Hyde Lea & Coppenhall WI, p110
Hodgson, F	Glaisdale & Lealholm WI, p25
Imp. War Museum	Photograph courtesy of the Imperial War Museum, London, Image negative No. MH4443, p111
Johnson, Eileen	Lumb in Rossendale WI, p49
Jones, P A	Gwynedd Caernarfon FWI, p32
Kenwright, E M	Colwall WI, p32
Kingsnorth, June	Ford WI p81
Knight, R M	Avon FWI p20
Leedham, Keith	Rayleigh WI, p19
Lloyd Jones, M	Gwynedd Caenarfon FWI p95
Lumsdale, Pat	NFWI stool p76, Work of Women in Wartime p7, cushion cover p69
Lydd WI	Lydd WI, p104
Meek, Anne	Wolviston Village WI, p78
Miller, Tom	Morton WI, p13
Mitchell, Ann	Cookham Afternoon WI, p24
Mitchell, S	Madron WI, p81
Morgan, Rosalie	Llangyfelach WI, p11
Norton, Susan	Bucks FWI Box p79, lace collar & needle case p71, Bucks map p105
Parker, Lois	Marnhull WI, p23
Pennington, Sylvia	Headley Woodlands WI, p83
Pettit, L T	Llanbister WI, p33
Portus, Julia	Humberside FWI, p57
Potter, Yvonne	Renhold WI, p18
Purser, J	Merstham WI, p42
Reed, Mary	Gwent FWI, p15
Rawlinds, Georgi	Nth Kelsey WI, p47
Richards, M	Painswick WI, p89
Riches, Beryl	Kingston Magma WI, p9
Roberts, Eva	Powys Montgomery FWI, p95
Roe-Barnett, W F	Eglwysfach WI, p98
Ruddick, Joan	Teesside Fed WI, p55
Sainsbury-Plaice, C	Sample books p40 & p72, lace samples p58, smock pattern sampler p62, cushion cover p62, apron p65, purse & two samplers p67, linen sampler p69, dress p70, guild of learners' badge and sample p70, cushion p77, tea cosy p78, cushion cover p62
Savage, J A	Colwall WI, p32
SC Studios, Essex	Essex FWI, p56
Slater, J A	Clayton le Woods WI, p93
Smith, Mary D	Scotton & District WI, p82
Swinley, M A J	Flaxley WI, p106
Thomas, Olive	High Wycombe WI, p20
Thornton Watlass WI	Thornton Watlass WI, p43
Trevennor, Wendy	Shrewton & District WI, p12
Tucker, Jean	Aston Ingham WI, p114
Walsby, C	Bengeo WI, p41
Weston, Jan	Peasmarsh WI, p82
Weston, S	Albury Evening WI, p31 & p85
Whatmore, P	Bledlow WI, p26
Williams, M	Melbury Osmond WI, p108
Willoughby, J A	Herts FWI, p76

Surrey FWI banner (detail)

Bedspread. 1924. Holmwood WI. Surrey

This bedspread was designed by Mrs Margaret Worrow and made by the members of Holmwood WI. It was made as a record of the founding of this Institute in 1920 and has the names of the 59 members embroidered on the panels. It was presented to the retiring first President, Mrs G. Barton, in 1924. After Mrs Barton's death, the cloth was given to Mrs Worrow, who had instigated the idea of the cover, and her son and daughter-in-law returned the cover to the Institute in 1986.

Linen bedcover with cut work and drawn thread techniques with filet crochet inserts and edgings